故園畫憶

庚寅中秋
韓馨逸 題

《故园画忆系列》编委会

名誉主任：韩启德

主　　任：邵　鸿

委　　员：(按姓氏笔画为序)

万　捷	王秋桂	方李莉	叶培贵
刘魁立	况　晗	严绍璗	吴为山
范贻光	范　芳	孟　白	邵　鸿
岳庆平	郑培凯	唐晓峰	曹兵武

故园画忆系列
Memory of the Old
Home in Sketches

鲁中漫记
A Sketch of Middle Shandong Area

刘婷婷　绘画 撰文
Sketches & Notes by Liu Tingting

学苑出版社
Academy Press

图书在版编目（CIP）数据

鲁中漫记 / 刘婷婷绘画、撰文. — 北京：学苑出版社，2015.10
（故园画忆系列）
ISBN 978-7-5077-4887-1

Ⅰ.①鲁… Ⅱ.①刘… Ⅲ.①钢笔画—作品集—中国—现代②山东省—概况 Ⅳ.①J224②K925.2

中国版本图书馆CIP数据核字(2015)第242256号

出版人：孟白
责任编辑：周鼎
出版发行：学苑出版社
社　　址：北京市丰台区南方庄2号院1号楼
邮政编码：100079
网　　址：www.book001.com
电子信箱：xueyuanpress@163.com
销售电话：010-67601101（销售部）、67603091（总编室）
经　　销：全国新华书店
印 刷 厂：北京信彩瑞禾印刷厂
开本尺寸：889×1194　1/24
印　　张：6
字　　数：145千字
图　　幅：123幅
版　　次：2015年11月北京第1版
印　　次：2015年11月北京第1次印刷
定　　价：45.00元

目　录

序　　　　　　　　　　王延松

前言

济南市

大明湖	3
趵突泉	4
黑虎泉	5
珍珠泉	6
五龙潭	7
兴国禅寺	8
灵岩寺	9
四门塔	10
长春观	11
吕祖庙三大殿	12
巡抚大院旧址	13
府学文庙	14
长清文庙	15
解放阁	16
大观园	17
李氏祠堂	18
瑞蚨祥布店	19
宏济堂药店	20
德华银行济南分行旧址	21
山东丰大银行旧址	22
北洋大戏院	23
济南老火车站	24
胶济铁路济南火车站旧址	25
济南市邮政局大楼	26
济南府电报收发局	27
齐鲁大学医学院	28
济南市京剧院	29
洪家楼天主教堂	30
基督教礼拜堂	31
清真北大寺	32
清真南大寺	33
泉城广场	34
曲水亭街	35
龙山黑陶	36
济南泥塑	37
鼓子秧歌	38
民俗彩灯会	39
千佛山庙会	40
木偶戏	41

淄博市

周村古商城	45
齐长城遗址	46
姜太公祠	47
颜文姜祠	48
蒲松龄书馆	49
蒲松龄故居	50

中国古车博物馆	51	坊茨小镇	79
殉马坑博物馆	52	杨家埠村	80
王渔洋纪念馆	53	甲子文化园	81
赵执信纪念馆	54	青州市博物馆	82
淄博市博物馆	55	诸城恐龙博物馆	83
青云寺	56	潍坊世界风筝博物馆	84
四世宫保砖牌坊	57	老龙湾	85
张店天主教堂	58	石门山	86
李家疃村	59	常山	87
峨庄民居	60	驼山	88
周村大街	61	沂山	89
聊斋城	62	泰和山	90
马踏湖	63	仰天山	91
莲花山	64	麻布绒绣	92
留仙谷	65	潍坊风筝	93
潭溪山	66	潍坊年画	94
马鞍山	67		
刻瓷	68	**泰安市**	
五音戏	69	岱宗坊	97
周村花灯	70	玉泉寺	98
		关帝庙	99
潍坊市		南天门	100
偶园	73	玉皇顶	101
十笏园	74	瞻鲁台	102
奎文门	75	唐摩崖	103
龙兴寺	76	碧霞祠	104
范公亭	77	孔子庙	105
潍县乐道院	78	五贤祠	106

汉明堂	107	**莱芜市**	
三阳观	108	莱芜战役烈士纪念塔	121
普照寺	109	苍龙峡	122
岱庙（一）	110	云台山	123
岱庙（二）	111	笔架山	124
岱庙（三）	112	剪纸	125
岱庙（四）	113	糖画	126
岱庙（五）	114	面塑	127
岱庙（六）	115	皮影戏	128
岱庙（七）	116	山东草编	129
东岳庙会	117	莱芜梆子戏	130
		山东蓝印花布	131

Contents

Foreword   Wang Yansong

Prologue

Ji'nan City

Daming Lake	3
Spouting Spring	4
Heihu Spring (Black Tiger Spring)	5
Pearl Spring	6
Wulong Pond (Five Dragons Spring)	7
Xingguo Temple	8
Lingyan Temple	9
Simen Pagoda	10
Changchun Taoist Temple	11
Three Main Halls in Lüzu Temple	12
The site of Shandong Governor's Compound of Qing Dynasty	13
Fuxue Confucian Temple	14
Dacheng Hall in the Confucian Temple in Changqing County	15
Liberation Pavilion	16
Grand View Garden	17
The Li's Ancestral Temple	18
Ruifuxiang Cloth Store	19
Hongjitang Drugstore	20
Former Site of the Ji'nan Branch of Deutsche Asiatische Bank	21
The Old Foreign Bank of Ji'nan	22
Beiyang Theater	23
The Old Ji'nan Railway Station	24
Ji'nan Station on Jiaozhou-Ji'nan Railway	25
Ji'nan Municipal Post Office Building	26
The Ji'nan government telegraph office	27
Medical School of Qilu University	28
Ji'nan Peking Opera Theater	29
Hongjialou Church	30
Christian Church	31
The North Mosque	32
The South Mosque	33
Spring City Square	34
Qushuiting Street	35
Longshan Black Pottery	36
Ji'nan Clay Sculpture	37
Guzi Yangko Dance	38
Folk Arts and Lantern Fair	39
Ji'nan Temple Fair in Mount Qianfo	40
Puppet Show	41

Zibo City

Ancient Business Block in Zhou Village	45
Ruins of the Great Wall of Qi	46
Master Jiang's Temple	47

Yan Wenjiang Temple	48
Pu Songling Private School	49
Former Residence of Pu Songling	50
China Museum of Ancient Carriages and Horses	51
Sacrificial Horses Pit Museum	52
Wang Yuyang Memorial	53
Zhao Zhixin Memorial.	54
Zibo Municipal Museum	55
Qingyun Temple	56
Brick Memorial Gateway of "Four Generations of Gong Bao (an official title in feudal China)"	57
Zhangdian Catholic Church	58
Lijia Tuan Village	59
Folk Houses in E'zhuang	60
Zhoucun Street	61
Liaozhai Park	62
Mata Lake	63
Lianhua Mountain	64
Liuxian Valley	65
Tanxi Mountain	66
Saddle Mountain	67
Engraved China	68
Five-tone Drama	69
Zhou Village Lanterns	70

Weifang City

Ou Garden	73
Shihu Garden	74
Kuiwen Gate	75
Longxing Temple	76
Fangong Parvillion Park	77
Weixian County Ledao Compound	78
Fangci Town	79
Yangjiafu Village	80
Jiazi Cultural Park	81
Qingzhou Municipal Museum	82
Zhucheng Dinosaur Museum	83
Weifang World Kite Museum	84
Laolong Bay	85
Shimenfang Mountain	86
Chang Mountain	87
Camel Mountain	88
Mount Yi	89
Taihe Mountain	90
Yangtian Mountain	91
Floss Embroidery on Sackcloth	92
Weifang Kite	93
Weifang New Year Pictures	94

Tai'an City

Daizong Archway	97
Yuquan Temple	98
Temple of Guan Yu	99
South Heavenly Gate	100

Yuhuang Peak	101	East Mountain Temple Fair	117
Zhanlutai Platform	102		
Cliff Monument of Tang Dynasty	103	**Laiwu City**	
Bixia Ancestral Temple	104	Monument for Martyrs in Laiwu Battle	121
Confucian Temple	105	Canglong Canyon	
The Temple of Five Sages	106	(Black Dragon Canyon)	122
Ming Hall of the Han Dynasty	107	Yuntai Mountain	123
Sanyang Taoist Temple	108	Bijia Mountain (Brushholder Mountain)	124
Puzhao Temple	109	Paper Cutting	125
Dai Temple (1)	110	Sugar Painting	126
Dai Temple (2)	111	Dough Modeling	127
Dai Temple (3)	112	Leather Silhouettes Show	128
Dai Temple (4)	113	Shandong Straw Plaited Article	129
Dai Temple (5)	114	Laiwu Bangzi Opera	130
Dai Temple (6)	115	Shandong Indigo Printed Sheeting	131
Dai Temple (7)	116		

序

  中国传统文化源远流长、博大精深。融合各族人民的智慧，用艺术的形式来弘扬传统文化，不仅要体现出对文化的外在表现，更重要的是挖掘其内在底蕴和丰富内涵。刘婷婷用一幅幅古建筑以及表现民俗文化的速写作品，让大家感受到她对传统文化的热爱与追求，充分表达出了历史文化的内在魅力。

  传统文化是文明演化而汇集成的一种反映民族特质和风貌的民族文化，是民族历史上各种思想文化、观念形态的总体表征。随着社会的变革与发展，有些人谈起传统文化来，总觉得有些虚无缥缈，遥远而不可触摸。其实不然，它就在我们身边，每一座古建筑都蕴含着丰富的历史内涵，每一种民俗文化都体现着中华民族特有的精神与气息，与我们的生活息息相关，而文化的个性也深深的根植于我们的民族血液之中。从这点意义来说，绘制一本具有历史记忆的画作，对于唤起人们对传统文化的保护意识具有积极作用。

  刘婷婷的速写不仅仅为了表现物象本身，更注重其精神内涵和理念，以及自己思想和内心的情感流露。她的速写讲究形与形的互相呼应，画面元素的互相衬托，注重建筑风格的特色捕捉，让人有不同层次的视觉张力的享受。在她的画作中，体现了她对古建筑文化的热爱与深刻理解，运用娴熟的绘画技巧重塑了古建筑的精神韵味，轻逸中渗透着历史厚重感。在这一幅幅生动的画作中，我们可以看到济南、泰安、淄博等地的古建筑，体现了鲁中地区不同历史时期的建筑风格，虽历经岁月的洗礼，仍屹立在齐鲁大地，体现着自己的价值，记载历史的同时也是中华文明的精神载体，给人一种宁静幽寂、气韵生动、形神具备之美感；而皮影戏、年画、赶庙会等独具特色的民俗文化，更是千百年来百姓生活智慧的结晶和生活传统，体现了人们对幸福生活的执着追求，一幅生动而古朴的人文风情画面跃然眼前。

  悠悠岁月在时光的空隙中渐渐沉淀下来，穿越中华民族上下5000年的记忆，不屈的中国传统文化在传承之路上屹立不倒，历经代代坎坷，却依然绽放光芒。

  让我们跟随这本画册，走进源远流长的文化长河中，从每一座建筑中，从每一个故事里，去体验齐鲁文化的风采与情怀，感受历史赋予我们的文化精神与民族魂，领略传统文化的无穷魅力。

王延松
2015 年 3 月

Prologue

The Chinese culture has a long, extensive and profound history. To express traditional Chinese culture in the form of art, the artists not only have to present its external manifestation but also dig deep into its core to present its rich cultural deposits.

When talking about traditional culture in a modern context, some may feel that it is too abstract or far removed from everyday life but such is not the case. Culture infiltrates every part of our life. Every historic building contains rich historic deposits and each folk tradition presents a spirit that is unique to the Chinese nation. This unique culture runs deep in our blood. From this perspective, an album of paintings with historic memories helps to awaken general awareness and protect traditional Chinese culture.

Portrayed in the vivid paintings by the artist Liu Tingting are the ancient buildings in Ji'nan, Tai'an and Zibo, among others which show the different styles of architecture in middle Shandong area at different stages of history. Through the test of time, these buildings still stand proudly and firmly bearing the history and civilization of the Chinese nation. The portraits of folk arts such as leather-silhouette show, New Year pictures and temple fair are the fruit of the common people's wisdom. They show the people's unending and unwavering pursuit of happiness.

Time is frozen in the album. After 5000 years, the traditional Chinese culture is still alive and well. Although it has many ups and downs, it still shines.

Let us travel within this album and journey to the world of traditional Chinese culture. Let us feel the touch of the ancient Shandong culture in every building and every story. Let us feel the spirits of the Chinese nation and the wonderous attraction of traditional Chinese culture.

Wang Yansong
March 2015

前 言

我出生在山东济南，深受着齐鲁文化的滋养。儿时的记忆，司空见惯了老城中历史建筑的壮美与沧桑，习以为常了民间艺人走街串巷、敲锣打鼓的叫卖和表演，一切是那样的自然。一座城市不施粉黛，安详地等待人们静静品味她的美，仿佛时间都为此而变得缓慢了些。

时光流逝，如今的城市面貌悄然发生着质的变化，那些历史悠久的建筑被拔地而起的高楼所包围，渐渐淡出了人们的视野。儿时民间艺人的叫卖声被汽车笛鸣声淹没，消失在了历史的洪流中。然而，那些巍巍然、屹立不倒的老建筑，依然是历史最具说服力的见证者，也是岁月留给我们的瑰宝。它们像一位位老者述说着一段段城南往事，勾起人们星星点点的回忆。

这次有幸参与学苑出版社的《故园画忆》项目，也给了我一个探求山东历史文化精髓的契机。通过对鲁中不同地域文化的了解，使我丰富了对历史文脉、建筑文化、风土民情等方面的认识。

在《鲁中漫记》的绘制中，我尽量去当地亲身体会不同建筑形式和民族风俗带给人的强烈感染力，并运用速写平实、放松、质朴的线条，抒发内心最原始的情感，描绘出建筑真实的面貌。也希望借以此书，和大家一起追忆那尘封已久的历史情怀。

由于本人艺术语言还不够纯熟，表现手法较为稚拙，还请广大读者给予批评指正。

Foreword

I was born in Ji'nan, Shandong province and have been nurtured by Shandong's culture. As long as I can recall, I was moved by the magnificent and weather-beaten historic architecture in the old city. I was fascinated by the folk artists that wandered around alleys and streets, giving performances to the beat of drums and gongs. It has always been completely natural to me.

As time rushes by, the cities have gone through gradual but fundamental changes. The ancient buildings are surrounded by mushrooming high-rises, and the folk artists' cries are drowned out by honking cars. However, those stately old structuress remain the most convincing witnesses of the region's rich history.

I am very lucky to be part of *Memory of the Old Home in Sketches* program sponsored by the Academy Press. This program gives me an opportunity to search for the essence of the history and culture of Shandong province. By looking into the different cultures in different regions of Shandong, I have obtained a more thorough understanding of Shandong's history, architecture and local customs.

When preparing for A sketch of Middle Shandong Area, I tried to visit the places I was going to paint in order to feel atmosphere and appeal of different forms of architecture and local customs. I use the plain and relaxed lines of sketch to express the most primitive feelings inside me and present the buildings as they are. Through this album, I hope to recollect the historic sentiments that have been long buried in the rubble of history and share them with you.

The language of my art might not be as sophisticated a form of expression as it is uncomplicated but this album is created from my heart and I am looking forward to your comments.

济南市
Ji'nan City

大明湖

位于老城区北部,现历下区明湖路,面积约46万平方米,济南三大名胜之一,素有"泉城明珠"之美誉。历史悠久,湖名见诸文字已有1400多年,其集水域风光、古园林景观、名胜古迹周匝其间。湖水来源于城内珍珠泉、濯缨泉、王府池等诸泉,有"众泉汇流"之说。清代书法家铁保留下的"四面荷花三面柳,一城山色半城湖"的名句,道出了大明湖的神韵。

Daming Lake

Located in the north of the old city in downtown Ji'nan, Daming Lake is one of the top three tourist attractions in Ji'nan. It is known as the "Pearl of the Spring City." "Lotus all sides and willows three, A Town of mountain, half of lake." This famous poem describes the charm of Daming Lake.

趵突泉

　　位于历下区，是泉城济南的象征与标志，与千佛山、大明湖并称为济南三大名胜。清代康熙皇帝南游时，观赏了趵突泉，兴奋之余题了"激湍"两个大字，并封为"天下第一泉"。泉水四季恒定在18摄氏度左右，严冬时节，水面上水气袅袅，像一层薄薄的烟雾，构成了一幅奇妙的人间仙境。

Spouting Spring

Located in the Lixia District of Ji'nan, Spouting Spring was firstly built in 1956 as a symbol of Ji'nan, the Spring City. Emperor Kangxi of the Qing Dynasty (1644-1911) granted it the title of "The Finest Spring under Heaven." The temperature of the spring water is approximately 18℃ year round.

【黑虎泉】

　　位于历下区泉城广场东部，与济南城的护城河相连。早在金代以前就已闻名于世。泉源处于悬崖下深邃天然洞穴中。水清澈见底，寒气袭人。洞口由青石垒砌，内有巨石盘曲伏卧，犹如猛虎深藏。泉水从巨石下涌出，湍击岩石，发出震天的鸣响。夜半朔风吹入石隙裂缝，惊人的吼声在洞中回荡，酷似虎啸，故名黑虎泉。

Heihu Spring (Black Tiger Spring)
Located in the east side of Spring City Square in Ji'nan, Heihu Spring has been famous in the country since before the Jin Dynasty (1115-1234). The spring water gushes from under a giant rock, striking the rocks and making thundering noises.

【珍珠泉】

　　位于历下区泉城路。泉池长42米、宽29米。泉水清澈如碧，一串串白色气泡自池底冒出，仿佛漂撒的万颗珍珠，迷离动人；泉的西北角有濯缨池，是由泉水汇聚而成，泉水向北流经百花洲后进入大明湖。

Pearl Spring

Located in the center of the old city of Ji'nan, Pearl Spring is as clear as jade. It runs north through Baihuazhu Islet into Daming Lake.

五龙潭

位于老城西门外，现历下区趵突泉北路，泺源桥北，南临趵突泉，北接大明湖。潭周名泉众多，形成五龙潭泉群。据《水经注》记载，北魏以前就有这片水，称净池。相传五龙潭昔日潭深莫测，每遇大旱，祷雨则应，故元代在潭边修建庙宇，内塑五方龙神，故此得名"五龙潭"。五龙潭公园内，散布着形态各异的 26 处古名泉，构成济南四大泉群的五龙潭泉群。

Wulong Pond (Five Dragons Spring)

Wulong Pond is located outside the West Gate of the old city of Ji'nan. Around the Pond 26 famous springs are scattered in various shapes. Inside the temple built by the pond in Yuan Dynasty (1206-1368), there are five sculpted dragons which is how the spring got its name.

兴国禅寺

兴国禅寺坐落于千佛山山腰，南是峭壁，北面泉城。寺院为千佛山主体建筑，青瓦红柱，花窗棂扉，殿宇亭廊结构错落，院内植有银杏、红枫、翠柏、椿树。明朝刘敕曾作《咏兴国寺》诗，对它做过全面地描绘："数里城南寺，松深曲径幽。片湖明落日，孤障插清流。云绕山僧室，苔浸石佛头。洞中多法水，为客洗烦愁。"

Xingguo Temple

The picture shows Xingguo temple in the Mount Qianfo, located in the Mount Qianfo mountain, the south is a steep, Northsprings.Mount Qianfo monastery is the main building, the red column tiles. The Ming Dynasty Liu Chi was "chant poems on Xingguo Temple", it made a comprehensive description.

灵岩寺

地处泰山西北麓，因殿内供置众多佛像得名。始建于唐贞观年间（627～649年），宋嘉佑年间（1056～1063年）和明嘉靖年间（1522～1566年）、万历年间（1573～1620年）重修，现存木结构为明代建筑。其面阔七间，进深四间，单檐庑殿顶。檐下置疏朗宏大的斗拱，木棱彩绘华丽，檐角长伸高耸，有展翅欲飞之势。前檐下立有八根石柱，柱础皆雕刻有龙、凤、花、叶、水波及莲瓣、宝装荷花等纹样，雕工精美，凸显唐宋之风。图为灵岩寺的千佛殿。

Lingyan Temple

Pictured is the Hall of Thousand Buddhas in Lingyan Temple. Located on the northwest slope of Mount Tai, the Hall got its name for the large number of Buddha statues enshrined in the hall. It was initially built in the Tang Dynasty and the existing wood structure was from the Ming Dynasty. The carvings here are particularly exquisite.

> 四门塔

　　位于历城区柳埠镇，建于隋代，距今已有 1400 年了。是中国现存唯一的隋代石塔，也是中国现存最早、保存最完整的单层庭阁式石塔。为全石结构佛教塔，每边宽 7.4 米，高度略同面宽，呈平面四方形。用当地出产的大青石砌成，非常坚硬，1000 多年来尚无风化侵蚀的情况。

Simen Pagoda

Located inside the Shentong Temple in Liufu Township, Licheng District of Ji'nan,,Simen Pagoda is 1400 years old. It is the only existing stone pagoda from the Sui Dynasty (581-618) and is the oldest and most intact single-story stone pagoda in the pavilion style in all of China.

长春观

位于市中区长春观街 1 号。始建于北宋政和元年（1111 年），历代多次重修，现存为清代所建。主要有大殿、东西配殿、东西厢房、后阁楼及丘子洞，丘子洞拱形门上方写有隶书"长春洞"三字，其在历史上一直是道教的重要活动场所。

Changchun Taoist Temple

Located at No.1 Changchunguan Street, Ji'nan, the Changchun Taoist Temple was first built in 1111. The current building was rebuilt during the Qing Dynasty (1644-1911) and has been an important venue for Taoism.

> 吕祖庙三大殿

位于历下区趵突泉公园内。坐北朝南，起于趵突泉池北岸。由两座楼阁和一座后殿组成，合称三大殿，占地约 1000 平方米。三大殿是一组较大的明清建筑，最南第一大殿为涑源堂，面对泉池，临岸直起，高二层，面阔三间，进深一间，高架两层，歇山飞檐。红漆木楹柱，黄色琉璃瓦，金碧辉煌，蔚为大观。

Three Main Halls in Lüzu Temple

Located inside the Sprout Spring Park, it is a complex that was built during the Ming (1368-1644) and Qing Dynasty (1644-1911). The southern-most hall is a two-story building about three jian wide and one jian deep, south facing toward the spring pond.

> 巡抚大院旧址

位于历下区珍珠泉东侧，建于清康熙五年（1666年），由山东巡抚周有德拆青州明衡王府大殿木料建造。昔时为清山东巡抚及民国山东军政首脑施政、断狱的场所。面阔五间，进深四间，歇山九脊，翘角飞檐，前为卷棚式，六根大红柱。红柱之间，为落地槅扇，檐角脊端，皆饰吻兽。

The site of Shandong Governor's Compound of Qing Dynasty

Located to the east of the Pearl Spring, the Compound was built in 1666. It is about five jian wide and four jian deep with nine-ridge gable, hip roof, and unwrapping corners and overhanging eaves. (Translator's note: jian is a unit of measurement in traditional Chinese architecture, referring to the distance between two main supporting columns. The exact length may vary.)

[府学文庙]

位于历下区明湖路248号。始建于宋代，清代多次修整，但基本保持了明朝文庙的规模和建筑布局。建筑群规模宏大。

Fuxue Confucian Temple

Located at No. 248, Minghu Road, Lixia District, Ji'nan, Fuxue Confucian Temple was initially built during the Song Dynasty (960-1279) and renovated multiple times during the Qing Dynasty (1644-1911). The temple has retained the scale and layout of the Confucian Temple of the Ming Dynasty(1368-1644).

{长清文庙}

位于长清区清河街499号，是古时教育机构。图为长清文庙之大成殿，始建于宋代，现存整体结构主要是清代的。大殿座北朝南，单檐庑殿顶，面阔七间，进深四间，比例结构上采用的古代官式做法。

Dacheng Hall in the Confucian Temple in Changqing County

Located at No. 499, Qinghe Street, Changqing District, Dacheng Hall was initially built in the Song Dynasty (960-1279) but its existing structure is well preserved and dates mostly from the Qing Dynasty. The Hall is approximately 7 jian wide with hip roof and single eaves.

> 解放阁

　　位于老城城墙东南角，现历下区下河涯街。阁址曾是1948年济南战役人民解放军攻克济南时的攻城突破口。旧城城墙因城市建设而拆除时，特意在此建起了巍峨壮观的解放阁，以纪念济南解放。解放阁是济南标志性的建筑之一。

Liberation Pavilion

Located in the southeast corner of the defensive walls of the old city of Ji'nan, Liberation Pavilion is one of the landmarks of Ji'nan. The site was the breach point where the People's Liberation Army conquered Ji'nan during the 1948 Battle of Ji'nan.

【大观园】

位于市中区经四纬二路十字路口。建于1932年，距今已有70多年的历史。按照南京夫子庙、上海城隍庙古建筑风格进行修建，形成灰瓦、白墙、红柱的外观景象，这种遵古模式极力还原了大观园的老商埠特色。

Grand View Garden

Located at The crossroad of Jingsi Road and Wei'er Road and built in 1932, the over-70-year-old Grand View Garden has gray tiles, white walls and red columns, which are classical elements of Chinese architecture..

李氏祠堂

　　位于章丘市绣惠镇茂李村南，当地人称之为家庙。据李氏家谱得知，李氏从元至正二年（1341年）迁至此地，李家祠堂始建于明代，清代多次重修。整个祠堂院落南北长100米，东西宽22米，分前后两院，主要建筑是一间坐北朝南的大殿和门楼。

The Li's Ancestral Temple

Located south of Maoli village of Xiuhui township, Zhangqiu city, the Li's Ancestral Temple was called by the locals as "Family Temple." It was first built duirng the Ming Dynasty (1368-1644) but there is only one courtyard left. The temple has a front and a back yard with the main buildings being the big hall and the gatehouse.

| 瑞蚨祥布店 |

位于槐荫区经二纬三路口附近。清同治元年（1867年），瑞蚨祥创始人孟鸿升最先在济南院西大街（今泉城路）路南设立了"瑞蚨祥"，经营绸缎、绣货和布匹等。孟鸿升创立的"瑞蚨祥"连锁商号极富盛名，至今仍是北京、天津、济南、青岛等地的著名老字号商店。他成为中国北方最大的民族商业资本家。

Ruifuxiang Cloth Store
Located near the intersection of Jing'er Road and Wei'san Road, Ruifuxiang is a cloth store founded in the Qing Dynasty (1644-1911), selling silk fabrics, embroidery and cloth amongst other goods.

| 宏济堂药店 |

　　创办于清光绪三十三年（1907年），创办人是同仁堂创办者的后人乐敬宇。历经近百年的风雨，已不再是单纯的一个药店、一座老建筑，它已成为见证历史、承载人们联想和记忆的重要文物。图为宏济堂西号的正面，其主要吸取了西式建筑风格，而室内布局则是传统的中式手法。在济南中西合璧建筑中最具代表性。

Hongjitang Drugstore

Founded in 1907, Hongjitang Drugstore has been through over a hundred years of ups and downs. The exterior of the building draws on western architectural styles while its interior decoration adopts the traditional Chinese style. This makes it the best representation of the combination of Western and Chinese architectural elements.

德华银行济南分行旧址

位于槐荫区经二纬二交叉路口东北侧,建于清光绪二十七年(1901年),德华银行,建筑至今保存完整。建筑主体为二层,局部三层。主屋面顶部的小望楼和八角形塔楼均为双层变折式屋顶,其高低、大小、位置有所差异,从而形成了丰富多彩的建筑竖向形象。

Former Site of the Ji'nan Branch of Deutsche Asiatische Bank

Located at the crossroad of Jing'er Road and Wei'er Road, the Ji'nan Branch of Deutsche Asiatische Bank was built in 1901 as the first foreign bank in Ji'nan invested by German businessman. The building has a rich mixture of architectural attributes.

山东丰大银行旧址

位于槐荫区纬六路27号。始建于1919年，曾任北洋政府总理的潘复等人在济南成立丰大银行其建筑面积600平方米，是济南商埠区保存较完整、具有南欧巴洛克风格建筑的孤本，承载着济南商埠的独特文化，为丰富商埠欧式建筑风格具有重要意义。在济南近代史上，人们也习惯以"老洋行"称呼它。

The Old Foreign Bank of Ji'nan

Located at No. 27 Wei'liu Road, the former Shandong Dafeng Bank was built in 1919 in a bold Baroque style. In the modern history of Ji'nan people refer to it as "the Old Foreign Bank."

> 北洋大戏院

位于槐荫区经二纬三路通惠街1号,始建于1905年,是山东省历史最为悠久的戏剧演出场所之一,至今仍在使用。许多著名表演艺术家如程砚秋、侯宝林、马季等都曾在此演出。该剧院在海内外梨园界和广大戏迷中享有较高声誉。

Beiyang Theater

Located at No. 1 Tonghui Street between Jing'er Road and Wei'san Road, Beiyang Theater was built in 1905 and is one of the oldest theaters in Shandong province. The theater is still in use today.

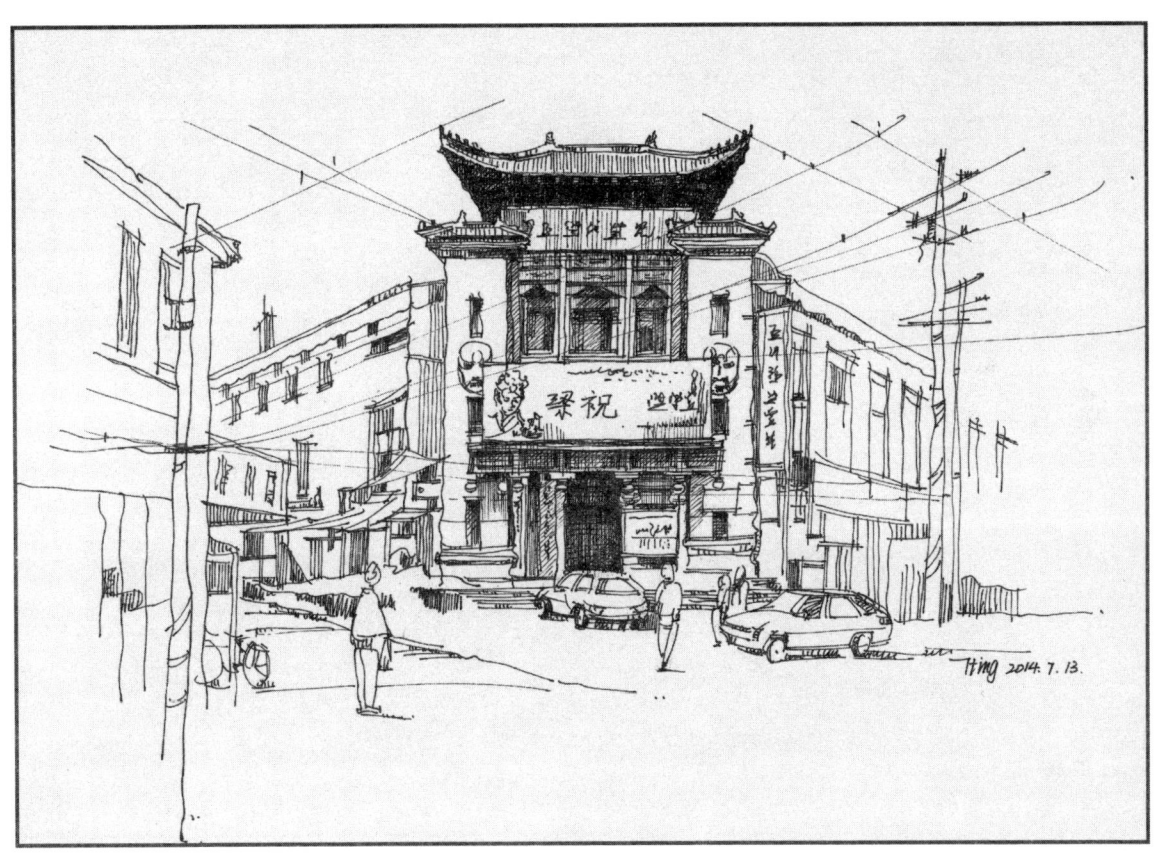

济南老火车站

位于槐荫区经一路北侧,指津浦铁路济南站,是19世纪末、20世纪初德国著名建筑师赫尔曼·菲舍尔设计的一座典型的德式车站建筑。曾是亚洲最大的火车站,它见证了济南这座城市在中国近代史中的沧桑岁月。1992年拆除,此图根据老照片绘制。

The Old Ji'nan Railway Station
Located on the north side of Jingyi Road of Jinan, the Old Ji'nan Railway Station is a classical German-style railway station. It was once the largest railway station in Asia. The building was demolished in 1992.

胶济铁路济南火车站旧址

位于天桥区车站街东侧,欧式建筑。清光绪三十年(1904年)动工,1915年建成。该建筑为一字形平面,主入口位于中间偏东部分并稍向南突出,通往候车大厅。门洞二层为石柱廊,有六根高大粗壮的爱奥尼石柱。今为济南铁路办事处。

Ji'nan Station on Jiaozhou-Ji'nan Railway

Built in 1915, Ji'nan Station on Jiaozhou-Ji'nan Railway is a European-style building on the east side of Chezhan Street in the Tiaoqiao District, Ji'nan city. The building has an in-line façade with six tall and thick Ionic columns.

济南市邮政局大楼

位于槐荫区经二路。1919年，由天津外国建筑师事务所建筑师查理及康恩赛设计，瑞典人纳自敦主建。占地约6705平方米，外墙红砖加以石料点缀，建筑三层。木制地板，复式红瓦房顶。即便是在今天，矗立在多座摩天大楼的旁边，邮政局大楼依然展示自己的魅力。

Ji'nan Municipal Post Office Building

Located on Jing'er Road in the old commercial port of Ji'nan, the Ji'nan Municipal Post Office was built in 1919. The outer walls of the 3-story building were made of red bricks decorated with aggregated rocks. It has wooden floors and multiple red-tile roofs.

济南府电报收发局

位于经一路与车站街的交汇处西北角。建于1904年，采用巴洛克建筑风格，呈两翼基本对称的格局，北翼为柜台和电报室、设备室等，西翼为办公用房，二层为办公和住宿用房，中部设圆柱形角楼。砖石混合结构，墙体部分为内砖外石。

The Ji'nan government telegraph office

The telegraph office was firstly built in 1904 in a bold Baroque style, the building is located in the road and Station Street in the northwest corner of the intersection. the original is the basic pattern of symmetrical wings, as the north wing of the counter and telegraph room, equipment room, West Wing office space, two storey office and residential buildings, the middle part is provided with a cylindrical turret, with brick mixed structure, brick and stone wall part.

齐鲁大学医学院

位于历下区文化西路。始建于 1865 年，由英国、美国和加拿大三国基督教会所创办。历经百年风雨，仍有不少古建筑得以幸免，在一代代师生的精心保护下，作为教学、科研、办公和住宿用房继续发挥着重要的作用。

Medical School of Qilu University

Located on the Wenhuaxi Road of Ji'nan, the Medical School of Qilu University was built in 1865 by the Christian churches of Britain, America and Canada. After a century of rain and storms there are still a number of old buildings that have survived.

> 济南市京剧院

　　位于槐荫区经二路 168 号，建于 1932 年。曾为山东省民生银行所在地。建于 1932 年。建筑上繁下简，以竖向手法为主，挺拔有力，顶承三角形大山花，北立面六根带有爱奥尼克柱头的方形巨柱，庄重华丽。

Ji'nan Peking Opera Theater

Located at No. 168, Jing'er Road, the building was formerly the site of Minsheng Bank of Shandong Province. It was built in 1932. The building is complicated on the top and simple in the lower part with mostly vertical lines. On the north façade there are six giant square columns with Ionic chapiters.

洪家楼天主教堂

　　为济南的标志性建筑物之一，也是济南文化带的重要象征。位于济南市区东部，历城区洪楼广场北侧，东邻山东大学老校，以洪家楼村而得名。教堂为双塔哥特式建筑，始建于1901年，是中国三大天主教堂之一，整个建筑气势宏伟，威严高耸，蔚为壮观。

Hongjialou Church

As one of Ji'nan's landmark buildings, but also an important symbol of Ji'nan's culture. The church is located in the east of Ji'nan, north of Hong Lou Plaza, Licheng District, east of the old school to Shandong University, named after the village of hongjialou. The church is Twin Towers Gothic architecture, was founded in 1901, is one of the three famous Chinese Catholic Church.

基督教礼拜堂

位于槐荫区经四路425号。始建于1924年,1926年落成。坐北朝南,平面为"工"字形,主体建筑高两层,底层为毛石砌墙,二层以上为清水红砖墙、红瓦顶,色彩鲜艳明快,立面造型质朴庄重,以文艺复兴时期建筑手法为基础,并融合了中国传统建筑部分形式,与整个商埠地区西式建筑的设计风格相融合。

Christian Church

Located at No. 425, Jingsi Road, Huaiyin District, Ji'nan, Ji'nan Christian Church is a two-story building facing the south first built in 1924. The building adopts the construction techniques of the Renaissance Age and integrates some of the skills used in traditional Chinese architecture.

> 清真北大寺

　　位于市中区西关永长街北端。始建于明弘治年间，历经沧桑、几经兴衰。建筑规模宏伟，风格独具。主体建筑大门、礼拜大殿、望月楼、配殿等，排列在一条东西中轴线上，南北讲堂对称，其建筑格式均为中国宫殿式古典建筑形式，同时还体现了阿拉伯建筑艺术特色，院内古柏点缀环境。

The North Mosque

Located at the north end of Yongchang Street, Xiguan, Ji'nan, the North Mosque is one of the most famous mosques in the country. First built sometime between 1488 and 1506, the grand mosque combines classical Chinese architecture with elements of Arabic architecture.

清真南大寺

俗称礼拜寺，位于市中区永长街南口，始建年代不详。是融合了中西建筑文化的大型伊斯兰教建筑群，为中国伊斯兰教早期著名清真寺之一。在建筑功能设置、朝向、内殿的装饰等方面都严格遵循伊斯兰教的一些基本原则，而在布局和造型上则有着明显的中国传统建筑的特点。全寺以望月楼为中心，为二进式四合院，严肃整齐，充分体现出中国传统四合院对称之美。

The South Mosque

Located at the south end of Yongchang Street, Shizhong District of Ji'nan, the South Mosque is one of the most famous early mosques in China. The year of its initial construction remains unknown. Centering on the Wangyue Building, the building complex is divided into two quadrangle courtyards that demonstrate the art of symmetry in traditional Chinese quadrangle courtyards.

泉城广场

位于市中心繁华地带，即历下区泺源大街，东西长 780 米，南北宽 230 米。广场东部是以荷花为造型的音乐喷泉，广场中心位置有 38 米高的主体雕塑《泉》，似三股清泉自"城"中磅礴而出，内涵丰富而直冲云天的挺拔造型。

Spring City Square

Located in downtown Ji'nan, the Spring City Square is 780 meters long from east to west and 230 meters wide from south to north. On the square there is a lotus-shaped music fountain and a main sculpture 38-meters high.

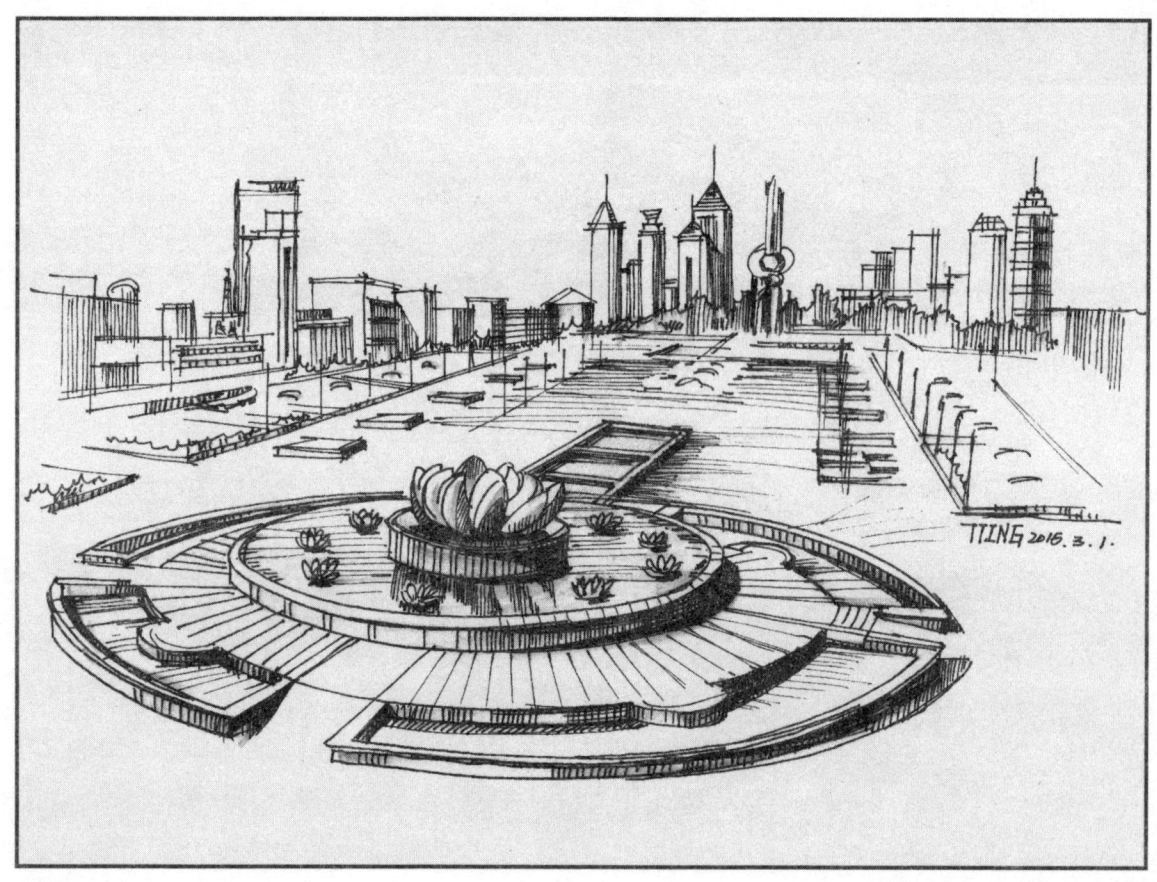

曲水亭街

　　位于历下区，是济南著名的老街。北靠大明湖、南接西更道、东望德王府北门、西邻济南府学文庙。一边是青砖碎瓦的老屋，一边是绿藻飘摇的清泉，临泉人家在这里淘米濯衣、垂钓品茶。依然完整地保留着《老残游记》中"家家泉水，户户垂杨"的泉城风貌。

Qushuiting Street

Located to the south of Daming Lake, Qushuiting Street is a famous street in Ji'nan. What you see are the old buildings with gray bricks and tiles on the one side and clear springs with green alga on the other. Residents nearby may be washing rice and clothes, sipping tea and fishing by the spring.

| 龙山黑陶 |

位于章丘市。龙山黑陶距今约四五千年，1928年首次发现于章丘龙山镇城子崖，史学家称之为"原始文化的瑰宝"。采用高温渗碳方法自然烧制而成，具有"黑如漆、亮如镜、硬如瓷、声如磬、薄如纸"等特点，尤其黑陶中的蛋壳陶，壁厚仅为0.3毫米，最薄处仅有0.1毫米。

Longshan Black Pottery

Longshan is located in Zhangqiu city of Ji'nan. Longshan Black Pottery has a history of approximately four to five thousand years. It is made by carburization in high temperature. The walls of the "egg-shell pottery" are only 0.3 mm thick with the thinnest part at only 0.1 mm.

[济南泥塑]

　　传统的民间艺术。以泥土为原料，以手工捏制成形。或素或彩，以人物、动物为主。泥塑是古代人类文化智慧的结晶，分布黄河上下、大江南北。各地的泥塑均具有强烈的地区特色。

Ji'nan Clay Sculpture

Clay Sculpture is a traditional folk art. Clay is made into different shapes by hands. The clay sculptures are mostly in the shape of people or animal and may be colored or plain.

> 鼓子秧歌

　　流行于济南一带的古老的汉族民间舞蹈。最初发源于商河县，有2000多年的历史。据记载，祝河竣工，民众自发鼓伞齐舞以示庆贺。后演变成民间为庆丰收而载歌载舞的汉族民间艺术。每年的元宵节是演出活动的高潮日。

Guzi Yangko Dance

It is an ancient folk dance in the Han nationality in Ji'nan area to celebrate a good harvest with drums, umbrellas and dances. It has a rich history of over 2000 years. The climax of its performance comes each year at the Lantern Festival.

民俗彩灯会

　　每年在春节之后拉开帷幕，凸显了老济南的民风民俗。将老济南的集市、梨花大鼓、茶艺、龙舟赛等民间活动和农俗的七月七、乞巧节、中元节、花朝节、龙抬头等节日集中体现出来，热闹非凡。

Folk Arts and Lantern Fair

The Folk Arts and Lantern Fair is held right after the Spring Festival each year. It presents different folk art activities such as the old market of Ji'nan, Lihua Drum (a popuplar entertainment in which the singer sings folk songs to the accompaniment of drum by herself), the art of tea, dragon boat regatta, and others. It is a busy and lively fair.

| 千佛山庙会 |

　　汉族民俗活动。自元代开始，定于农历九月九日为千佛山庙会。每年重阳佳节，人们要到千佛山登山，站在"赏菊岩"上赏菊。庙会期间，从山脚到山腰兴国禅寺的山路两旁，全是吹糖人的、捏面人的、卖冰糖葫芦的、唱戏的、说书的、拉洋片的，热闹非凡。

Ji'nan Temple Fair in Mount Qianfo
It is a traditional folk custom for the Han nationality set on the ninth day of the ninth month in the lunar calendar since the Yuan Dynasty (1206-1368). People will climb Mount Qianfo and appreciate chrysanthemum blossoms on "Chrysanthemum Appreciation Rock" in the Double Ninth Festival.

> 木偶戏

汉族传统戏剧，古称傀儡戏。历史悠久、品种繁多、技艺精湛。人以木偶为媒介，"以歌舞演故事"。木偶造型多数沿用戏曲中的生旦净末丑等戏剧脸谱，表现不同的人物形象。演员在幕后一边操纵木偶，一边演唱，并配以音乐。根据木偶形体和操纵技术的不同，有布袋木偶、提线木偶、杖头木偶、铁线木偶等。

Puppet Show

Puppet show is a traditional drama of the Han nationality. The puppets often use the facial makeup as in the Chinese opera. The artists control the puppet from behind the scene while singing along.

淄博市
Zibo City

周村古商城

位于周村区西部。唐宋时期，周村商业初具雏形，主要由大街、丝市街、银子市街、绸市街、芙蓉街等古街区组成。街道两侧建筑风格迥异，且至今仍在发挥其商业功能，是山东省境内唯一保存较完好的明清古建筑群。

Ancient Business Block in Zhou Village
Located in the west of Zhou Village, it is the only well-preserved ancient building complex from the Ming and Qing Dynasty in Shandong province. The commerce in Zhou Village began to take shape in the Tang (618- 907) and Song Dynasties (960-1279). The buildings along the streets are widely different in style and are currently still in use.

| 齐长城遗址 |

　　齐长城，始建于春秋时期，比秦长城早 400 余年，距今已 2500 余年。司马迁《史记·楚世家》中载："乘山岭之上筑长城，东至海，西至济洲，千余里以备楚。"源于济南市长清区孝里镇广里村，古济水河东岸，从大峰山山顶通过，蜿蜒千里，直达青岛市黄岛区东于家河村北入海，全长 619 千米，共翻越 1518 座山峰。图为齐长城的残存碉楼。

Ruins of the Great Wall of Qi

The Great Wall of Qi is now over 2500 years old. It starts from the Guangli village of Xiaoxi Township, Changqing District, Ji'nan City, zigzagging for 619 kilometers. It crosses over 1518 peaks to reach the sea at the north of Yujiahe Village, east of Huangdao District of Qingdao City.

姜太公祠

位于临淄城区。1993年，以姜太公衣冠冢为依托而建，是一组中国传统的中轴对称、殿堂庙宇建筑。祠内分为六个院落，亭台楼阁、曲折回廊。姜太公是中国历史上著名的政治家、军事家、谋略家，是周代齐国的第一代国君，被历代帝王尊封为"武圣"，民间传太公为神上神。

Master Jiang's Temple

The temple is located in downtown Zibo city. It is a traditional Chinese temple with axisymmetric layout. Master Jiang was a well-known politician, militarist and strategist during the late Shang Dynasty (1600-1046 BC) and early West Zhou Dynasty (1046-771 BC). Legend holds that Master Jiang was the "God of Gods."

> 颜文姜祠

又名顺德夫人祠，俗称大庙，位于博山区城郊西南境内凤凰山南麓。始建于北周，是仅存的三座唐代木质建筑物之一。全祠南北长 64 米，东西宽 61 米，主要建有山门、香亭、正殿、东西两庑、寝殿等计 73 间。整个建筑物规矩严谨，金壁交辉。

Yan Wenjiang Temple

Commonly known as the Big Temple, Yan Wenjiang Temple is located on the south slope of Fenghuang Mountain in the southwest suburb of Boshan District, Zibo City. Initially built in 557 A.D., the existing building complex is wooden and dates to the Tang Dynasty. It has 73 rooms, including the front gate, the incense pavilion, the main hall, rooms on the east and west side facing the main hall, and bedrooms.

蒲松龄书馆

位于周村区西南昆仑路旁，原系明末户都尚书毕自严故居的一部分。蒲松龄32岁时在此设馆教塾，71岁高龄时才撤帐归里田园，其著名的小说《聊斋志异》及大量诗词皆出于此。

Pu Songling Private School

Located in southwest of Zhou Village, Zibo City, Pu Songling (1640-1715) was a famous writer in Qing Dynasty who began his teaching career here at the age of 32. He wrote the famous collection of short stories "Strange Tales of a Lonely Studio" and many poems from this house.

> 蒲松龄故居

　　位于淄川区洪山镇蒲家庄。其著作《聊斋志异》家喻户晓、誉满中外。蒲松龄故居是一座幽静古朴的庭院，院落坐北朝南，故居门前是几株古槐，荫翳天日。北院正房三间，为蒲松龄的诞生处和其书房"聊斋"。

Former Residence of Pu Songling

The residence faces the south. In the north courtyard there are three principal rooms, which is where Pu was born and his study "Liaozhai (Lonely Studio)"

> 中国古车博物馆

　　位于临淄区齐陵镇后李官庄，是当代中国最系统、最完整，以车马遗址与文物陈列融为一体的古车博物馆。以1990年全国十大考古发现之一的后李春秋殉车马坑为基础而建，分为古车陈列馆和地下春秋殉车马展厅两大部分。

China Museum of Ancient Carriages and Horses

Located in Houliguan Village, Qiling Township, Linzi District, the Museum has two parts.The Exhibition Hall of Ancient Carriages and the underground exhibition hall of Houli Sacrificial Carriages and Horses.

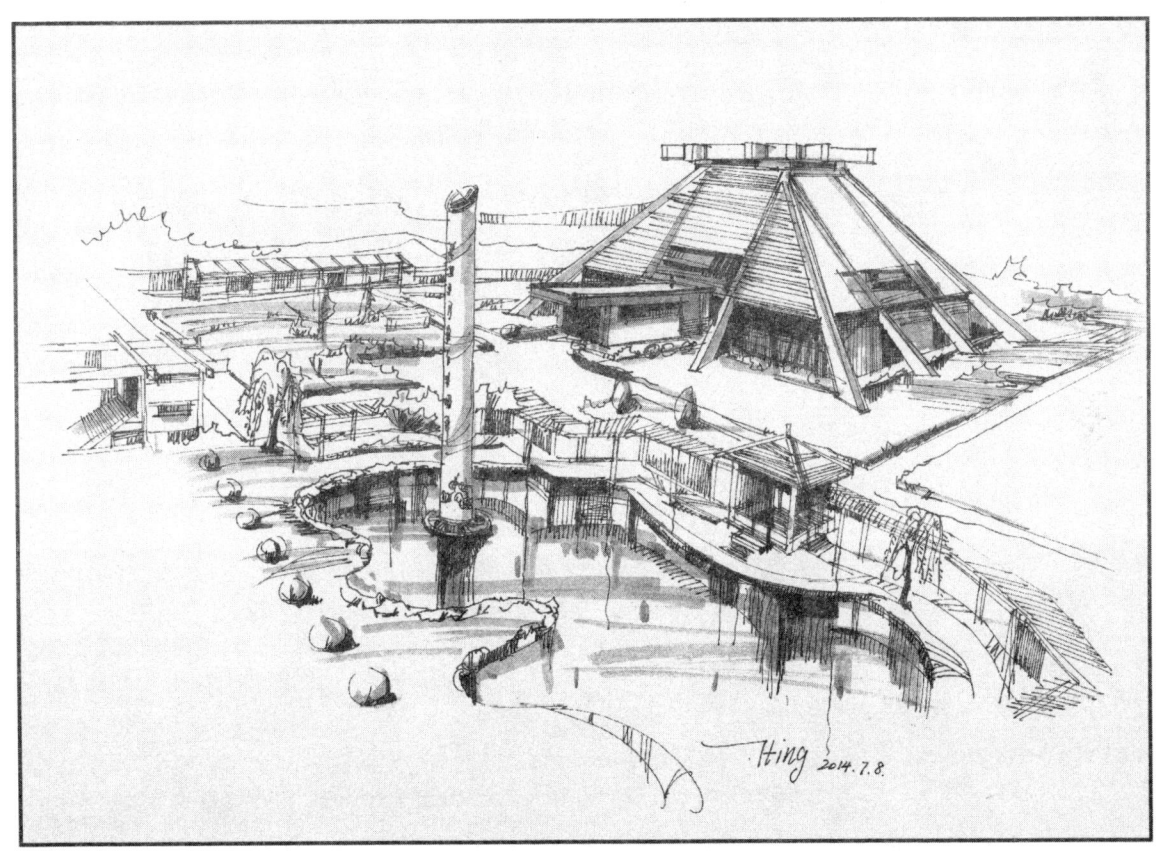

> 殉马坑博物馆

位于临淄区河崖头村西。建于齐国执政最长的国君齐景公的墓地上。墓早年被盗，随葬品无存，唯周围的殉马坑大部分保存完好。殉马全是壮年战马，马两行，前后叠压，昂首侧卧，四足蜷曲，形作奔跑状，呈临战姿态，威武壮观。全部殉马当在600匹上下，属世界罕见。

Sacrificial Horses Pit Museum

Located in the west of Heyatou Village, Lizi District, Zibo City, the Museum was built at the original site of the sacrificial horse pit of Duke Jing of Qi (547-490B.C.) There are approximately 600 sacrificial horses, all of which were war horses duirng the prime of their lives. They are staged in the running position, ready for battle.

> 王渔洋纪念馆

　　位于桓台县新城镇的忠勤祠内，为纪念清代刑部尚书王渔洋而建。整组建筑系砖木结构，分东西主跨两院，保持了典型的明代建筑风格。馆内设七个展室和石刻园。

Wang Yuyang Memorial

Located in Xincheng Township, Hengtai County, Zibo City, the Memorial was built in memory of Wang Yuyang, a respected poet and Minister of Punishments in the Qing Dynasty. It is located in the Shrine for Loyalty and Diligence, which is a building from the Ming Dynasty built in 1588. The Memorial has seven exhibition rooms and a stone inscription garden.

| 赵执信纪念馆 |

位于博山区中心路东首,坐落于博山的古代园林因园旧址上。为清代风格的四合院,清康熙二十四年(1685年)建造。其背依荆山,下临秋谷,山岩重叠,泉水绕屋。1994年重建,并建赵执信纪念馆,以纪念这位卓有成就的现实主义诗人、诗论家、书法家。赵执信,清代诗人,号秋谷。

Zhao Zhixin Memorial

Located in the East end of Zhongxin Road, Boshan District, Zibo City, this Memorial was built in memory of Zhao Zhixin, a realist poet, critic, and calligrapher.

淄博市博物馆

坐落在淄博市中心广场，是一座综合性博物馆。现有馆藏文物2.3万多件，以战国商王墓和西汉齐王墓地出土的青铜器、玉器、金银器最具代表性。

Zibo Municipal Museum

Located on the central square of Zibo city, Zibo Municipal Museum is a comprehensive chorographic museum. The museum has a collection of over 20,000 pieces of cultural relics featuring bronze ware, jade ware, gold and silver ware from the West Han Dynasty (202 BC-25AD) and the Age of Warring States (770-221 BC).

【青云寺】

位于淄川区岭子镇,在盘山、九纹山的幽谷中。为原淄川县八大寺之一,四山环合,景色秀丽。《淄川县志》载:僧人圆明,于西南山中创建青云寺者也。据此可知,寺已有550多年历史。

Qingyun Temple

Located in Lingzi Township, Zichuan District, Zibo City, the over-550-year-old Qingyun Temple is one of the eight temples of the former Zichuan county. Mountains enclose from all sides giving the Temple beautiful views of the surrounding scenery.

| 四世宫保砖牌坊 |

　　位于桓台县新城镇南村大街北端，建于明万历四十七年（1619年），青砖石灰砌成，工艺精妙、古朴典雅。是为表彰当时兵部尚书王象乾保卫明朝有功而建造。建坊时，王象乾正在兵部任内，时年71岁。当时，曾追封其祖上三代，因此该坊被称为"四世宫保"坊。石匾额"四世宫保"四字传为明代书法家董其昌书。

Brick Memorial Gateway of "Four Generations of Gong Bao (an official title in feudal China)"
Located in the north end of Nancun Street, Xincheng Township, Hengtai County, Zibo City, the Memorial Gateway was built with grey bricks and lime in 1619.

张店天主教堂

位于淄博火车站东北侧,初建于19世纪末。高30米,东西宽12米多,南北长40米,属于典型的哥特式建筑,几何线条明晰流畅,各部分尺寸比例搭配合理。高耸的尖顶钟楼配以挺拔的十字架,显示出欧式建筑的优美和浓厚的宗教色彩。

Zhangdian Catholic Church

Located in northeast of Zibo Railway Station, the Church was first built at the end of the 19th century. It is a typical gothic architecture, 30 meters high, over 12 meters wide from east to west and 40 meters long from south to north.

| 李家疃村 |

位于周村区王村镇东南。19世纪初，李家疃村有很多人到南方做绸缎、布匹生意，买卖兴隆，财源亨通，所赚银两大多用于买土地、建房屋。当时最豪华的建筑是九座不同形式的庭院，建在村庄的中轴线上，南北贯通，九门相冲，房屋宽敞高大，造型美观。

Lijia Tuan Village

Lijia Tuan Village is located in southeast of Wangcun Township, Zhoucun District, Zibo City. In the early 19th century, many villiagers in Lijia Tuan villiaged headed south to do business. They spent their earnings mostly purchasing land and building houses. The most extravagant buildings at the time were nine courtyards in different forms on the central axis of the village.

峨庄民居

　　位于淄川区东南部，是传统的鲁中民居。房屋大多依山而建，层次分明、错落有致。各村都留有大量的古房子和古树，另有石碑、字刻等文物。如今的峨庄古村民居依旧保持着古老典型的北方山区村庄风貌。

Folk Houses in E'zhuang

There are many old houses and old trees in the villages in the southeast part of Zichuan District, Zibo City along with cultural relics such as stone tablets and inscriptions.

周村大街

周村，享有"天下第一村"之称，现为周村区。周村大街总占地面积为60.5公顷，主要由大街、丝市街、银子市街等古街组成，现有保存完好的明清古建筑5万余平方米。景区内古迹众多，街区纵横，店铺林立，建筑风格中西文化合璧，且至今仍在发挥其商业功能。

Zhoucun Street

Zhoucun is one of Shandong District of Zibo city. Zhoucun street, covers an area of 60.5 hectares, mainly bystreet, city street, Silver City Silk Street Street, the existing well preserved ancient buildings in Ming and Qing Dynasty more than 5 square meters. Scenic spots in the numerous monuments, street shops, architectural styleaspect, combination of Chinese and Western elements, and still play its commercial function.

【聊斋城】

　　位于淄川区洪山镇蒲家庄。蒲家庄是清代小说家蒲松龄的故里。聊斋城是以聊斋故事为主题的大型名园,其蒲松龄故居较为完整地保留了当年的原貌。

Liaozhai Park

Located in Pujiazhuang Village, Hongshan Township, Zichuan District, Zibo City, Liaozhai Park is a theme park featured in the strange tales in Pu Songling's famous story collection "Strange Tales of a Lonely Studio." Pu Jiazhuang is the hometown of Pu Songling, a novelist in the Qing Dynasty.

> 马踏湖

位于桓台县境东北部，小清河南岸。马踏湖素有"北国江南、鱼米之乡"誉称。春秋时齐景公、三国诸葛亮、唐代李白、宋代苏东坡、元代于钦等官宦名人均至马踏湖游览。

Mata Lake

Located on the south bank of Xiaoqing River in the northeast of Hengtai County, Mata Lake is known as "South in the North", and "Land of Fish and Rice."

莲花山

　　位于泰沂山脉中段，有诗赞曰："蕊突瓣环似莲花，岭重峰叠却是山"。主峰犁铧尖海拔994米，其下山谷数条。其西北侧的大沟，峰高壑深。峪中溪流四季常流，飞瀑与激流、清泉与山涧相交融。

Lianhua Mountain

Located in the middle of Tai-Yi Mountains, Lianhua Mountain has several valleys with great views. Its main peak, Lihuajian (the tip of plough share), is 994 meters in altitude.

> 留仙谷

位于淄川城东郊的洪山镇五松山东侧,山水自然景观。东西走向,九曲十八弯,当地百姓称为九曲崖,全长约1500米,谷深100余米,谷中奇峰突兀,瀑布流泉、深沟绝壑、林密奇秀,是北方罕见的自然地质文化遗产。

Liuxian Valley

Located in the east suburb of Zichuan County, Liuxian Valley stretches from the east to the west with numerous turns and bends. The valley is over 100 meters deep with lofty peaks and roaring waterfalls.

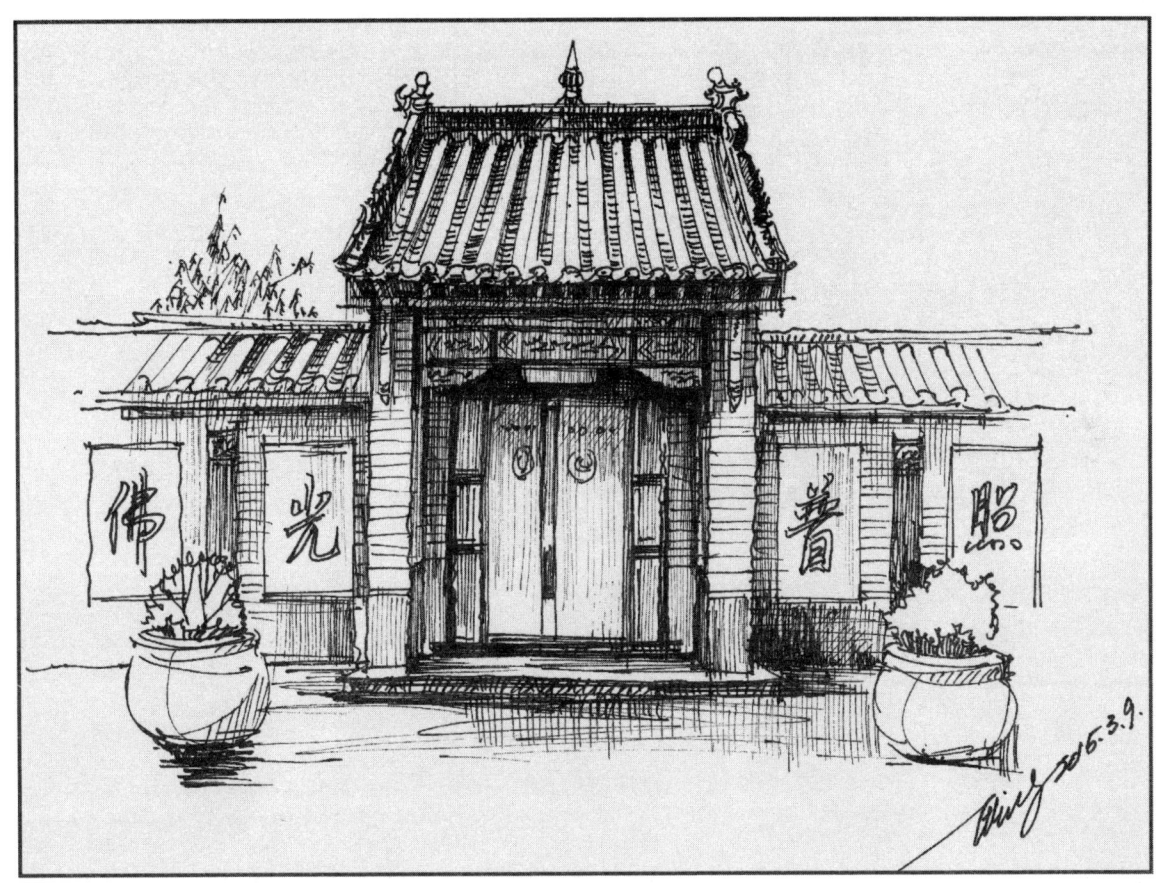

> 潭溪山

　　位于淄川区太河镇峨庄。最高海拔867米，森林覆盖率达80%以上，是得天独厚的"天然氧吧"。春赏山花烂漫，夏聆溪水潺潺，秋醉满山红叶，冬观银装素裹。

Tanxi Mountain

Tanxi Mountain is located in E'zhuang Village, Taihe Township, Zichuan District. The highest peak is 867 meters in altitude. The forest coverage rate is over 80%. Visitors can appreciate flowers in the spring, listen to the brooks in the summer, admire the red leaves in the autumn and enjoy the snow in the winter.

> 马鞍山

　　位于淄川区东南部淄河镇，因其形似马鞍而得名。这里峰峦叠嶂，是一个由粗犷雄伟的山峦、潺潺的溪流、波光粼粼的水域、秀丽多姿的田园山庄组成的自然风景区。主要景点有纪念馆、战斗遗址、怪石林、钟鼓楼、华光寺等。

Saddle Mountain

Located in Zihe Township southeast of Zichuan County, Saddle Mountain got its name for its shape. The mountain area is blessed with numerous peaks, cliffs and streams as well as a number of tourist attractions such as memorial hall, bizarre rocks, bell tower, drum tower, and Huaguang Temple among others.

[刻瓷]

汉族传统艺术，通常也指在瓷器、瓷板上刻凿成的雕塑工艺品。用特制刀具在瓷器、瓷板表面刻划、凿镌各种形象和图案。

Engraved China

It is a traditional art form of the Han nationality. The artists use special knives to engrave different patterns on the surface of chinaware.

| 五音戏 |

山东地区的独有汉族戏曲剧种，有200多年的历史。源于章丘、历城一带。原名肘鼓子戏，唱腔优美动听，语言生动风趣，表演朴实细腻，地方特色浓郁。由于方言、风俗等差异，大致划分为东、西、北三路。东路和北路渐趋衰微，只有西路被一支专业的戏曲团体承续下来，即今日的淄博市五音戏剧院。

Five-tone Drama
It is a type of drama exclusive to the Han nationality in Shandong province. It originates from Zhangqiu and Licheng area with a history of over 200 years. The Drama featured beautiful melodies and witty lyrics with special local characteristics.

周村花灯

周村元宵挂灯有悠久历史。春秋战国时周村叫於陵邑，当地百姓都养蚕织绸。每到正月十六日天后娘娘的生日，人们要祭祀教授人们养蚕织绸的黄帝的夫人嫘祖。人们起早包饺子放鞭炮，日出前在河里把蚕帘子洗刷干净。于是周村沿河两岸十五夜间便出现了两行长长弯弯曲曲的灯笼，逐步形成了正月十五闹社火，挂灯的风俗。

Zhou Village Lanterns

In the evening of the 15th day of the first month on the lunar calendar every year, residents of Zhou village would light the lanterns so that they can wash the bamboo trays for breeding silkworms in the river because they had to make sacrifice to the goddess governing the silkworm breeding the next day. The tradition of lighting lanterns and performing club fire activities on the 15th day of the first lunar month was passed down through the generations.

潍坊市
Weifang City

> 偶园

位于青州市里偶园街中段东侧。当地人称为"冯家花园",原是清初大学士兼刑部尚书冯溥的私人花园,系清康熙初年所建,是中国幸存的为数不多的"康熙风格"的园林建筑。结构严谨,亭阁棋布,怪石嶙峋,曲径通幽,竹柏森森,花木隐翳。

Ou Garden

Located on the east side in the middle part of Ou Garden in Qingzhou City, Ou Garden was built in the early days of Qing Emperor Kangxi's reign (1662-1722). It is a Kangxi-style garden, which is rare in China, with various pavilions, bizarre rocks and nagi.

十笏园

　　位于潍城区胡家牌坊街中段,是中国北方地区的汉族古典园林袖珍式建筑。始建于明代,园中的砚香楼原是明嘉靖年间(1522～1566年)刑部郎中胡邦佐的故宅。后于清光绪十一年(1885年)被潍县首富丁善宝以重金购作私邸,修葺了北部三间旧楼,题名砚香楼,开挖水池,堆叠假山,始成私人花园。

Shihu Garden

Located in the middle of Hujia Paifang Street, Weifang City, Shihu Garden is a small, classical garden in the architecture of the Han nationality. It was a private garden first built in the Ming Dynasty with black bricks and grey tiles in a brick-wood structure.

| 奎文门 |

位于奎文区白浪河畔。潍坊古城的城门，始建于明代，现存建筑为1988年复建。历史上的潍坊，四周由城墙包围，留有若干门供人出入。后旧城墙逐渐没落。所幸历经沧桑变故的奎文门穿越漫漫时空依然耸立在城市的中心，连同曾经斑驳、残破的旧城墙被时代赋予了更加鲜活的生命力。

Kuiwen Gate

Located on the bank of Bailang River, Kuiwen Gate is the gate of the old city of Weifang. It was initially built in the Ming Dynasty and the existing building was built in 1988. In the old days, Weifang city was enclosed by walls on all sides with several gates as entrances and exits.

龙兴寺

位于青州市，始建于北魏时期，是一处延续千余年的著名佛教寺院。龙兴寺的佛教造像窖藏是迄今中国发现的、数量最多的窖藏佛教造像群。它代表了自北魏至宋元时期中国佛教艺术的杰出成就。

Longxing Temple

Located in Qingzhou City, Longxing Temple was a Buddhist temple first built in the Northern Wei Dynasty (368-534). Its cellar storage of Buddhist sculptures is, by far, the largest in China.

> 范公亭

位于青州城西门外的小盆地里，因范仲淹惠政青州而得名。园内溪流蜿蜒、湖水潋滟、楼台参差、花木隐翳。范公亭为六角形，顶开一圆孔，与井泉上下相对，其亭之柱上木下石，别具风格。园内有数棵千年的唐楸、宋槐，还有翠竹千竿。

Fangong Parvillion Park

The Park is located in the small basin outside the western gate of Qingzhou City. Inside the park are meandering streams, a glittering lake, varied buildings and pavilions in addition to flourishing flowers and trees. There are also several Chinese catalpa and Chinese scholar trees from the Tang and Song Dynasty as well as thousands of bamboos.

| 潍县乐道院 |

位于老潍县东关，清光绪八年（1882年）前后由美国人建立，由教堂、学堂、医院组成。光绪二十六年（1900年）毁于义和团运动。光绪二十八年（1902年）北美长老会用"庚子赔款"在县城重建，使其得到了较大规模的发展，成为北美基督教长老会的山东总部。

Weixian County Ledao Compound

Located in Dongguan of the old Weixian county, the compound was built in 1882 by an American. It consists of three parts, a church, a school and a hospital.

坊茨小镇

位于坊子区。坊子区一带历史上以胶济铁路坊子段为中轴线两侧发展,彰显着潍坊近代工业文明进步的历史。近年由于煤矿采空、铁路改道等历史原因逐渐沉寂。但至今仍散落着大量带有德国、日本建筑风格的百年建筑。

Fangci Town

Fangci Town is located in Fangzi District of Weifang City. Historically, Fangzi District has been developed along the Fangzi section of Jiaozhou-Jinan railway. There are several buildings over-100-years-old in German and Japanese styles scattered around in this area.

| 杨家埠村 |

位于寒亭区，历史悠久，明古槐与明古屋、木版年画、风筝闻名遐迩。杨家埠民间艺术大观园为仿古建筑，四合院结构。内有杨家埠木版年画陈列馆、杨家埠风筝陈列馆、民俗院等。到这里可以亲手扎制风筝、套印木版年画，也可以放风筝，一饱民俗技艺之盛宴。

Yangjiafu Village

Located in Hanting District of Weifang City, the time-honored Yangjiafu Village is known for its old Chinese scholar tree and houses from the Ming Dynasty, Wood Engravings for the New Year and kites. Visitors can make kites or wood engravings by hand or just fly a kite.

> 甲子文化园

位于青州市的云门山与凤凰山下，以甲子文化为主题。建筑规模宏大、精美，包括无极殿、财神庙、城隍庙、甲子文化研究院、太岁宫和碑廊等。

Jiazi Cultural Park

Located at the foot of Yunmen and Fenghuang Mountains in Qingzhou City, the park has a number of grand and beautiful buildings, including Wuji Hall, Temple of the God of Wealth, and Town's God Temple among others.

青州市博物馆

　　位于青州市范公亭公园西端，为一座综合性博物馆。为古典式民族建筑群，建筑以回廊相连，厅廊均以金色琉璃瓦覆顶。收藏大量文物。

Qingzhou Municipal Museum

Located in the west end of Fan'gong Pavillion Park, it is a comprehensive chronographic museum with a large collection. The building complex is classical Chinese architecture.

诸城恐龙博物馆

诸城市以出土巨型鸭嘴龙化石而闻名,被称为"鸭嘴龙的故乡"。该博物馆展出目前世界上最高大的巨型鸭嘴龙化石骨架和100多件恐龙化石,是中国北方最大的恐龙博物馆。博物馆建筑风格独特,俯视似八条巨龙相抱互拥,平视似古埃及金字塔。

Zhucheng Dinosaur Museum
Zhucheng City is called "the hometown of Hadrosaur" because a large number of hadrosaur fossils that were unearthed there. Now the museum has a collection of over 100 pieces of giant dinosaur fossils and the largest giant hadrosaur fossil on exhibition.

| 潍坊世界风筝博物馆 |

建于 1987 年,是中国第一座大型风筝博物馆。建筑造型为龙头蜈蚣风筝的样貌,屋脊是一条完整的陶瓷巨龙。展出从公元前 5 世纪"鲁班风筝"至今的中外各式风筝千余件。

Weifang World Kite Museum

This large kite museum exhibits over 1000 kites from home and abroad, including the kite made by Luban, a famous craftsman in the fifth century B. C. The building is in the shape of a centipede kite with a dragonhead and the ridge is a complete porcelain dragon.

> 老龙湾

位于临朐县,弥河流域的上游地带。古称"薰冶湖",由地下泉水涌出地地表汇流而成,因传说湾内有泉眼直通东海并有神龙潜居其中而得名,泉水清澈见底,四季恒温18摄氏度,盛夏酷暑,清凉甘冽;数九隆冬,湾中云雾蒸腾,烟霞缭绕。

Laolong Bay

Located in Linqu County southwest to Weifang City, Laolong Bay was known as "Xunye Lake" in the ancient days. It was converged by the underground springs, the water is clear and the temperature remains at 18℃ year round.

石门山

位于临朐城西,山势曲结南向,两峰对峙如门。殷商临朐之城为逄国,石门山为逄国辖地。逄王为朝廷忠臣,人们为追念其功德,便在风景秀丽的石门山立庙祀之。到了唐代,增建庙宇,刻佛像,已成为名胜之地。宋元明时建成佛塔、神龛。清代、民国时期,续增摩崖刻石,新建文昌殿,构成了古代建筑群。

Shimenfang Mountain

Located in the west to Linqu City, Shimenfang Mountain stretches to the south with a history of 3000 years. In the Shang Dynasty (1600-1046 BC), Linqu was located in the State of Pang and Shimenfang Mountain was in its jurisdiction. Temples were built and Buddha sculptures were added later the place gradually turned into a cluster of ancient buildings.

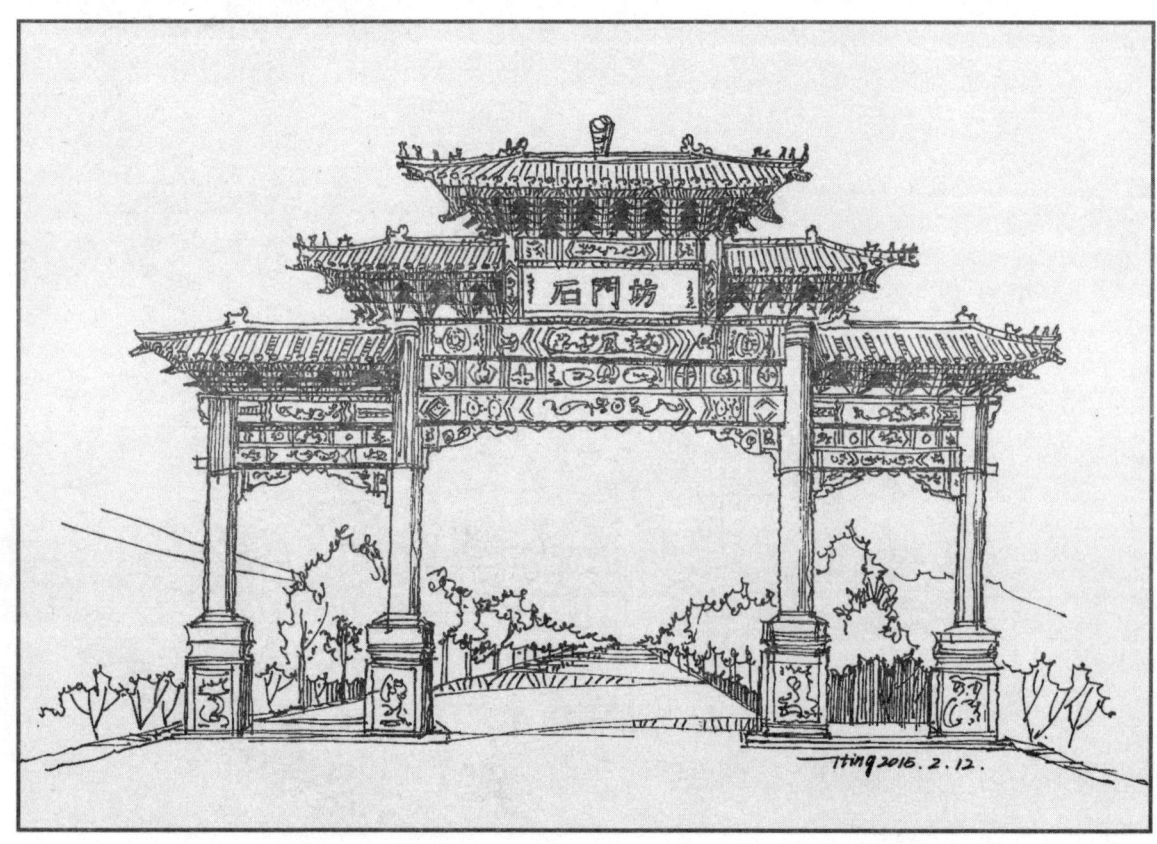

| 常山 |

原名卧虎山，位诸城市皇华镇西部，因形如卧虎而得名。山高297米，南坡多为悬崖陡壁。缓岗连绵，独常山突兀而起，加之山顶碧霞宫衬托，格外雄伟壮观。宋代大文豪苏轼曾多次登临此山，并写下了如《江城子·密州出猎》等诸多流传千古的诗文。

Chang Mountain

Located in the west of Huanghua Township, Zhucheng of Weifang City, Chang Mountain is 297 meters high. It is steep on the south slope and there is a magnificent Bixia Palace on the top. Su Shi, a great writer in the Song Dynasty (960-1127) visited the mountain on several occasions.

> 驼山

　　位于青州城西南 4000 米处，海拔 408 米，绵延数里，顶上双峰对峙，因像骆驼而得名。驼山有陡峭的山峰、古老的松柏以及盘桓而上的"天梯"及百余种动植物，还有为数众多的石窟造像和山顶的昊天宫等文物古迹。

Camel Mountain

Located 4 kilometers southwest to Qingzhou City, Camel Mountain is 408 meters high. Two peaks stand facing each other resembling a camel which is how the mountain was named. There are a great number of caves and Buddha sculptures in the mountain.

沂山

位于临朐县城，古称"海岳"，为"五镇"之一，素享"泰山为五岳之尊，沂山为五镇之首"的盛名。这里有以神龙大峡谷、狮子崮、歪头崮为代表的自然景观和以东镇庙、法云寺、玉皇顶等历史遗迹为代表的文化景观。

Mount Yi

Located in Linqu county of Weifang City, Mount Yi was called Haiyue, the Mountain on the Sea. On the beautiful and lush mountain, there are a number of historic sites, such as Dongzhen Temple, Fayun Temple and the Peak of the Heavenly Emperor.

泰和山

　　位于青州市西南山区庙子镇。峰恋叠嶂、碧水相依，集地貌、森林、人文景观于一体。天门、七峰联翠、看山狐、百鸟谷等自然景观引人入胜，100多种树木遍布山间。泰和山曾是明永乐年间（1403～1424年）农民起义军唐赛儿扯旗聚义的地方，在这里留下了大量的历史遗迹与优美传说。

Taihe Mountain
Located in Miaozi Township, in the mountainous area southwest to Qingzhou City
In Taihe Mountain, peaks rise one after another with streams running in the valleys. There are over 100 varieties of trees on the mountain. This was where the peasant rebel leader Tang Sai'er gathered his troops, leaving plenty of historic relics and legends.

> 仰天山

位于青州市西南46千米处,主峰海拔834米。山势雄奇、地貌怪异、森林遍布;寺院古老、文物丰富。自然景物与丰富的人文景观,相互融合,交相辉映。

Yangtian Mountain
Located 46 kilometers southwest of Qingzhou City, Yangtian Mountain is 834 meters high with bizarre landscapes, steep slopes and dense forests in addition to old temples with rich collections of cultural relics.

麻布绒绣

传统民间手工艺品。在特制的网眼麻布上,用彩色羊毛绒线,绣出各种画面和图案。历史上潍坊"九千绣花女"的盛大繁荣景象已难以寻觅。只有极少数人依然坚守着这古老的传统手工艺。

Floss Embroidery on Sackcloth

It is a traditional handicraft. The needlewoman uses colored wool floss to embroider all kinds of patterns on specially-made sackcloth. In the prime days, there were once 9,000 active needlewomen in Weifang.

> 潍坊风筝

民间传统手工艺玩具。风筝，古名"纸鸢"，制作普及山东各地，尤以潍坊为盛。潍坊风筝兴于明初的杨家埠村。那时，村民已有木版年画的刻印技术。他们利用每年春天的空余时间，用印年画的纸张、颜料，绘制出各种图案，扎制风筝。至清乾隆年间（1736～1795年）风筝已成为当地重要的手工业。

Weifang Kite

It is a traditional handicraft. Kite was called "paper glede" in the ancient times. Making kites is popular in every region of Shandong province, especially in Weifang. During the reign of Qing Emperor Qianlong (1736-1795), kite making has become an important handicraft industry in the area.

潍坊年画

　　民间美术工艺品,以杨家埠年画为代表,风行黄河下游一带。体裁广泛、想象丰富、重用原色、线条粗犷、风格纯朴。全以手工操作并用传统方式制作,始创于明末,清光绪年间(1875～1908年)达到鼎盛期。潍坊曾有"画店百家,画种上千、画版数万"之说。

Weifang New Year Pictures
It is a kind of folk art work represented by the New Year Pictures in Yangjiafu village. The pictures are all handmade in the traditional methods. In the past there were over a hundred galleries, over a thousand types of pictures and over 10,000 versions of painting in Weifang.

泰安市
Tai'an City

> 岱宗坊

　　位于泰山区岱宗大街。建于明嘉靖年间（1522～1566年），清代重建。岱宗坊建于泰山山脚下的石砌台基上，四柱三门式石坊，造型粗犷、简洁，额题篆书"岱宗坊"三个金色大字。

Daizong Archway

Located on Daizong Street, Daizong Archway is a four-column stone archway first built in the Ming Dynasty (1368-1644). The Archway has a bold and simple styling with three golden characters "Dai Zong Fang" written on the top in seal character.

玉泉寺

　　位于泰山北麓，始建于北魏，又称谷山寺。寺内有唐植银杏四株、大雄宝殿、一亩松、东西佛脚印、北魏石刻佛像等景观。以玉泉寺为中心，有大量佛教、民俗文化景观。

Yuquan Temple
Located on the northern slope of Mount Tai, Yuquan Temple, also known as Gushan Temple, was initially built in the Northern Wei Dynasty (386-534 AD) In the Temple there are four gingko trees planted in the Tang Dynasty, a giant pine tree whose crown covers 897 square meters as well as other attractions such as Buddha's footprints on both the east and west sides and stone carvings of Buddha from the Northern Wei Dynasty.

> 关帝庙

位于泰山登山古盘道起始处的西侧，属古建筑中的坛庙祠堂类，始建于明代。关帝庙座北朝南，共有三进院落，红墙青瓦。建筑依山就势层层叠起，布局错落有致。

Temple of Guan Yu

Located on the west side of the starting point of the climbing path of Mount Tai, the temple was initially built during the Ming Dynasty (1368-1644). The south-facing building has three courtyards with red walls and grey tiles.

| 南天门 |

 位于泰山上十八盘，在飞龙岩与翔凤岭之间的低坳处，海拔1460米。山于此为最危耸，上即绝顶。旧称三天门、天门关，由元中统五年（1264年）布山道士张志纯所建。门为阁楼式建筑，石砌拱形门洞。额题"南天门"。红墙点缀，黄色琉璃瓦盖顶，气势雄伟。

South Heavenly Gate

Located on the 18 bends of Mount Tai, the South Heavenly Gate, also known as the Third Heavenly Gate or the Heavenly Gate Pass, is 1460 meters in altitude. It is an attic-style building with stone doorway that was initially built during the Yuan Dynasty (1206-1368).

【 玉皇顶 】

　　为泰山主峰之巅，海拔 1545 米，气势雄伟，因峰顶有玉皇庙而得名。在此极目四望，确有"一览众山小"之感。玉皇庙始建年代无考，明成化年间（1465～1487 年）重修。主要建筑有玉皇殿、迎旭亭、望河亭、东西配殿等，殿内祀玉皇大帝铜像。神龛上匾额题"柴望遗风"，说明远古帝王曾于此燔柴祭天，望祀山川诸神。殿前有"极顶石"，标志着泰山的最高点。

Yuhuang Peak

It is the zenith of the main peak in Mount Tai with an altitude of 1545 meters. Looking into the distance from the Peak you may feel all the other mountains are belittled. The ancient emperors had made sacrifices here for the gods of mountains. There is a Yuhuang Temple on the peak with an unknown date of initial construction.

> 瞻鲁台

位于泰山上观峰南侧，俗称幡杆石。石梁突兀，平展如台，台上有巨石，上刻"瞻鲁台"三大字，寓意在此可远瞻鲁国曲阜。

Zhanlutai Platform

Located on the south side of Riguan Peak, Zhanlutai Platform and also known as Streamer Rod Stone, is an outreaching flat stone beam with three giant characters "Zhan Lu Tai" engraved on it, meaning "from here you can see the State of Lu in Qufu."

> 唐摩崖

　　位于泰山玉皇顶盘路东侧,俗称"大观峰"。崖壁上刻唐玄宗御制《纪泰山铭》,俗称唐摩崖碑。碑高 13.3 米、宽 5.7 米,碑文书 24 行。碑文为隶书。明代史学家、文学家王世贞评论说:"穿崖造天铭书,若鸾飞凤午于烟云之表,为之色飞"。

Cliff Monument of Tang Dynasty

Located on the east side of the path to Yuhuang Peak, the Cliff Monument is also known as Daguan Peak. On the cliff is engraved the Inscription to Honor Mount Tai written by Emperor Xuanzong of the Tang Dynasty. The monument is 13.3 meters tall and 5.7 meters wide with 24 rows of inscriptions.

| 碧霞祠 |

位于泰山极顶南侧，为古代高山建筑群。初建于宋代，原名昭真祠。由大殿、香亭等12座大型建筑物组成。建筑以照壁、南神门、山门、香亭为中轴 左右对称，南低北高，层层递进，布局严谨。

Bixia Ancestral Temple

Located on the south side of the summit of Mount Tai, Bixia Ancestral Temple is a mountain building cluster initially built during the Song Dynasty (960-1279). Originally known as Zhaozhen Ancestral Temple, the temple consists of 12 large buildings, including the Great Hall and the Incense Pavilion among others.

孔子庙

位于泰山岱顶望吴峰，海拔1472米处，是全国名山中唯一的儒家庙宇，是历代皇帝来泰山朝拜之处，以求"以文治国，国泰民安"。古人在岱顶建孔子庙，使圣人、圣山合二为一。庙内供奉孔圣人。建筑坐北朝南，由山门、正殿、东西耳房、东西配殿组成。

Confucian Temple

Located on the Wangwu Peak of Mount Tai at an altitude of 1427 meters, this Confucian Temple is the only Confucian temple built in the mountains. Emperors in ancient China would come here to worship the Mount Tai. The temple was built on the peak to unite the saint and the holy mountain into one.

五贤祠

位于泰山普照寺西北。祠东有投书涧，西有香水峪，溪水环流，山石林立。明嘉靖年间（1522～1566年）在此建祠，题额"仰德堂"，后增祀胡瑗，称三贤祠。至清道光年间（1821～1850年）徐宗干重修时，又增祀宋焘和赵国麟，遂易名五贤祠。

The Temple of Five Sages

Located northwest to Puzhao Temple, the Temple of Five Sages was built during the reign of Emperor Jiajing of the Ming Dynasty (1522-1566). In the east of the temple is Toushu Gully and in the west Xiangshui Valley. The temple was surrounded by streams and stone forest.

[汉明堂]

　　位于泰山脚下,北临碧霞湖。建筑古色古香、精巧别致,既有大汉遗风,又有明清古韵。由东膳房、书画院、仿汉乐舞演艺大厅、博物馆、茶艺馆及碑林五部分组成。周边荷塘月色、垂柳依依、小桥流水、曲径通幽。

Ming Hall of the Han Dynasty

At the foot of Mount Tai with Bixia Lake to the north, Ming Hall is of great antique beauty. It consists of five parts, including the east kitchen, the gallery of calligraphy and painting, Han-style performance art hall, museum, teahouse and stele forest.

> 三阳观

　　位于泰山的凌汉峰的山腰。这里松柏葱茂、麻栎蓊蔚、泉石铿然。明嘉靖三十年（1551年），东平道士王三阳携徒来此"伐木剃草，凿石为窟以居"。三阳观依山而建，东西宽60米，南北长90米。为三进院落，前院由山门、影墙、配房组成。山门之内天井甚阔，数株古柏银杏点缀其间，山门外道西有道士林，王三阳及其道徒墓和墓碑尚存。

Sanyang Taoist Temple

Located in the middle of Linghan Peak of Mount Tai, Sanyang Taoist Temple was built in 1551. It has three courtyards with several ancient gingko trees and cypress trees scattering around. The tombs and tombstones of Wang Sanyang and his disciples remain intact.

普照寺

位于泰山南麓的凌汉峰下。秀峰环抱,翠柏掩映亭殿楼阁。清人有"门前几曲流水,寺后千寻碧峰。鸟语溪声断续,山光云影玲珑"的赞咏。普照寺取"佛光普照"之意,传为六朝时建,后历代皆有拓修。寺院以双重山门、大雄宝殿、摩松楼为中轴线,形成三进院落,两侧配以殿庑、寮房、花园等。

Puzhao Temple

Located at the foot of Linghan Peak on the south slope of Mount Tai, Puzhao Temple was allegedly built in the Period of Six Dynasties (265-589 AD) and had been renovated constantly afterwards. The temple has three courtyards and two main gates.

岱庙（一）

又称东岳庙，位于泰山区，泰山南麓。图为岱庙的遥参亭。遥参亭是岱庙建筑群南北轴线上的一组建筑，实为岱庙的入口。历代帝王凡有事於岱宗，必先至此进行简单参拜，而后入庙祭神。"遥参亭"是岱庙的第一个景观，由于它的存在，把岱庙神秘而庄严的气氛烘托得更加浓厚，这种既独立又统一的建筑风格，不仅在五岳中独树一帜，在中国现存古建筑中也不多见。

Dai Temple (1)

Also known as Dongyue Temple, Dai Temple is located on the south slope of Mount Tai. In the picture is the Yaocan Pavillion, which is actually the entrance to Dai Temple.

岱庙（二）

　　图为岱庙的正阳门，古时只有帝王才能从此门进入。正阳门始建于宋，毁于20世纪中叶，现存是1985年重建的。正阳门高8.6米。上面的五凤楼高11米，共五间，为九脊单檐歇山顶，覆黄色琉璃瓦，24根四方明柱。两扇朱红大门上镶有81个铁制馒钉，象征着岱庙的尊严。

Dai Temple (2)

Pictured is the Zhengyang Gate of Dai Temple. In the ancient times, only the emperors were allowed to enter through this gate. It was initially built during the Song Dynasty and the existing gate was rebuilt in 1985. The door is 8.6 meters tall with 81 iron bun-shaped nails symbolizing the dignity of Dai Temple.

111

岱庙（三）

图为岱庙的唐槐院。旧称延禧殿院，院内唐槐高大茂盛，但民国年间枯死，后植新槐，今已扶疏郁茂，俗称"唐槐抱子"。树下有明代"唐槐"大字碑，又有清康熙年间（1662～1722年）的《唐槐诗》碑。院内遍植槐树，春夏之际满院飘香。百碑墙、古槐荫山、槐香池，再加上点缀其间的盆景，别有一番情境。

Dai Temple (3)

In the picture is Tang Huai Courtyard. The Chinese scholar tree from the Tang Dynasty used to be in the courtyard had died in the Republic years ( ) and the current tree was planted afterwards and has flourished with luxuriant foliage. Under the tree there is a stone monument from the Ming Dynasty with two Chinese characters engraved, reading "Tang Huai" and another stele with inscription of A Poem to Chinese Scholar Tree from the reign of Emperor Kangxi of the Qing Dynasty.

岱庙（四）

图为岱庙的天贶殿，"天贶"即天赐的意思。天贶殿是岱庙的主体建筑，主祀东岳大帝。相传北宋大中祥符元年（1008年）六月初六有"天书"降于泰山，宋真宗即于次年在泰山兴建天贶殿，以谢上天。天贶殿东西长44米，南北宽17米，殿阔九间，进深四间。整座大殿雕梁彩栋、贴金绘垣、丹墙壁立，虽经数朝，古貌犹存。

Dai Temple (4)

In the picture is the Tiankuang Hall. In Chinese, Tiankuang means "bestowed by heaven." Tiankuang Hall is the main building of Dai Temple, worshiping the God of Mount Tai. The original appearance remains although it has been through several dynasties.

岱庙（五）

图为岱庙的汉柏院。位于岱庙东南隅，院内原有炳灵殿，又有汉柏。院内巨匾高悬，有八角石栏水池。相传五株古柏为汉武帝所植。古人誉为"汉柏凌寒"，为泰安八景之一。

Dai Temple (5)

Pictured is the courtyard of cypress in the southeast corner of Dai Temple. In the courtyard a giant board hangs up high and there is a pool with an eight-cornered stone fence. It is thought that the five cypress trees inside the courtyard were planted by the Emperor Wu of the Han Dynasty (25-220 AD).

岱庙（六）

　　图为岱庙后院的铜亭。铜亭又名"金阙"，为明万历四十一年（1613年）铸。亭为铜质，施以鎏金，亭长4.4米，宽3.4米，内祀元君铜像。显示了我国古代精湛的冶铸工艺。

Dai Temple (6)
The copper pavilion is 4.4 meter long and 3.4 meters wide showing the fine melting and crafting techniques of ancient China.

岱庙（七）

　　图为岱庙后院的铁塔。铁塔为明嘉靖年间铸，造型质朴雄伟，原有13级，现仅存三级，原立于泰城天书观，1973年移此。

Dai Temple (7)
Pictured is the iron tower built during the Ming Dynasty. The iron tower had 13 stories but only 3 remain.

[东岳庙会]

又称泰山庙会,是古老的汉族民俗及民间宗教文化活动。缘起于泰山崇拜和道教在泰山的兴盛。滥觞于唐,定制于宋,鼎盛于明清。有商品交易、文娱活动,人们在这里购物、观赏、交流。

East Mountain Temple Fair

Also known as Mount Tai Temple Fair, East Mountain Temple Fair is an ancient folk custom and a religious activity for the Han dynasty. On the temple fair there are all kinds of trade, entertainment and cultural activities. Visitors can shop, sightsee and communicate there.

莱芜市
Laiwu City

莱芜战役烈士纪念塔

位于莱城区英雄路附近的黄山之巅，塔高19米，由泰山花岗石砌成，象征着在莱芜战役中牺牲的革命烈士们重如泰山。塔碑阳面"革命烈士纪念塔"七个鎏金大字是毛泽东的手迹，阴面为鎏金隶书碑文。

Monument for Martyrs in Laiwu Battle

Located on the top of Huangshan Mountain near Yingxiong Road in Laiwu city, the Monument is 19 meters high and is built with granite from Mount Tai, signifying that the martyrs who died in the Laiwu Battle are as significant as Mount Tai.

苍龙峡

位于莱芜城南,莲花山脚下。峡深数丈,两壁对峙,苍松翠柏,峡壁天然的溶洞,有的大如客厅,有的深不可测,怪石林立,极具观赏价值。每逢夏季大雨过后,洪水奔腾下泄,水雾冲起数丈之高,雷鸣之声响彻数里,这就是莱芜古八景之一的"苍峡雷鸣"景观,故古人有诗赞云:"不见浓云饰,殷殷丝雷鸣,岂知龙峡内,水势正奔腾"。

Canglong Canyon (Black Dragon Canyon)

Located at the foot of Lianhua Mountain south of Laiwu City, the canyon is quite deep with bizarre stones sticking out from the cliffs on the two sides. After the rainstorm in summer, the torrent roars down the valley making enormous thundering noises.

云台山

距莱城区 15 千米，海拔 578 米，主峰顶为平台，常有云雾缭绕山间。当地人称小泰山，传说山顶有泰山奶奶的行宫，山上一些庙宇仿泰山修筑和命名。中天门是小憩的好地方，在此南眺，夹谷峪一览无余，两面山势磅礴。山顶远望，泰莱平原，汶河西流，一览无余。

Yuntai Mountain

Located 15 kilometers away from Laiwu City, the Yuntai Mountain is 578 meters high. The peak is flat at the top covered with clouds and mist year round. The temples in the mountain are built and named after those in Mount Tai so Yuntai Mountain is known to the locals as the Little Mount Tai.

> 笔架山

　　位于莱芜市西南牛泉境内。相传东晋书圣王羲之曾云游至此，并与同僚畅饮"修禊"，因见此山形似笔架，顿生灵气，欣然提笔命名"笔架山"。属泰山山脉，山峰环抱，绿水环绕，各种树木满山遍野，一年四季郁郁葱葱。

Bijia Mountain (Brushholder Mountain)

Located in Niuquan Township southwest of Laiwu City, Bijia Mountain belongs to the Mount Tai ranges. Legend holds that Wang Xizhi, the reputable calligrapher in the Eastern Jin Dynasty (317-420), had visited here. He saw that the mountain looked like a brush-holder and delightedly picked up his writing brush and named the mountain "Brush-holder Mountain".

[剪纸]

民间手工艺品,又称窗花、窗染花、花儿等。工具是剪刀。题材有文字图案、鸟兽鱼虫、山水风景、民间传说等。这些题材和表现手法,在广大农村经几代民间艺人的承传、提炼、修改,创作出一大批构图严谨、造型优美、格调高雅的传统剪纸精品。

Paper Cutting

Also known as paper-cutting for window decoration or flowers, paper-cutting is a traditional handicraft. The craftsman cut the papers with scissors into different patterns, such as Chinese characters, birds, beasts, fishes, insects and landscapes as well as folk tales.

糖画

　　以糖为材料来进行浇铸造型的一种民间传统手工艺。所用的工具仅一勺一铲，糖料一般是红、白糖加上少许饴糖。糖料用温火熬制到可以牵丝后，艺人用小汤勺舀起糖料，在石板上飞快地来回浇铸成型。艺人的手上功夫便是造型的关键。当浇铸完成后，用小铲刀将造型铲起，粘上竹签，一副生动的糖画就完成了。

Sugar Painting

This traditional handicraft is made of sugar with a spoon and a slice. The artist scoops up a spoonful of melted sugar and paints different patterns on a piece of slate. The key is all on the hands of the artist.

> 山东草编

传统的农家手工产品,已成为著名的民间工艺品。以麦秸草、玉米皮、蒲草为原料最为普遍,产品丰富多样。

Shandong Straw Plaited Article

It was initially the handmade product of the rural families and gradually evolved into to a form of folk handicraft. There are a wide variety of straw plaited products made mostly from wheat straw, corn-husk and the stem and leaf of cattail.

> 面塑

俗称捏面人，民间传统手工艺。糯米面为主要材料，艺人使用小竹刀，将彩色糯米面手工制作成栩栩如生的人物、动物、植物，深受人们喜爱。

Dough Modeling

Commonly known as dough figuring, this traditional handicraft makes mostly sticky rice powder into vivid figures, animals, and plants, which are very popular.

【皮影戏】

　　汉族民间广为流传的傀儡戏之一。民间艺人运用牛皮、驴皮等，经过手工刀雕、彩绘制成人物、动物和场景的皮影。表演时，艺人在白色幕布后面，用手操纵皮影，同时用当地流行的曲调唱述故事，配以打击乐器和弦乐，具有浓厚的乡土气息。

Leather Silhouettes Show

It is one form of the puppet shows popular among the Han nationalities. The artists control the handmade leather silhouettes from behind a white curtain and sing to the accompaniment of instruments, which is of heavy with local flavor.

莱芜梆子戏

山东民间戏曲之一，已有200多年历史。其音乐具有鲜明的特色，唱腔高亢雄壮，旋律平实、行腔流畅，具有浓厚的乡土气息和独特的艺术魅力。以莱芜为中心的鲁中腹地，莱芜梆子曾是当地文化活动的主要形式，具有很强的凝聚力。

Laiwu Bangzi Opera
A folk opera with distinct local features, it has a history of over 200 years. Laiwu Bangzi Opera had been a main form of entertainment in the middle Shandong area centered on Laiwu.

山东蓝印花布

蓝印花布是用防染方法印染而成的,印花板过去采用油纸刻制。传统做法:豆浆、石灰、蛋清混合作为防染浆,透过印版刷在白布上,晾干后再用靛蓝水色煮染,待布干后刮去灰浆,呈蓝底白花,故被称为蓝印花布。蓝印花布色彩质朴、纹样丰富,蕴含吉祥寓意。

Shandong Indigo Printed Sheeting

The indigo printed sheeting is made with traditional dyeing technique with white patterns on an indigo background. The patterns are diversified with auspicious implication, which made it very popular in the past.